IN THE ARMS OF
MARY

Thirty-One Days with Our Blessed Mother

Fr. Emmanuel Okami & Lisa Timms

© 2020
Fr. Emmanuel Okami & Lisa Timms

ISBN:
979-868-653-011-9

IMPRIMATUR
Bishop Ayo Maria Atoyebi, OP
Bishop Emeritus of Ilorin Diocese, Nigeria.

NIHIL OBSTAT
Very Rev. Fr. Stephen Audu
Ilorin Diocese, Nigeria.
Resident at St. Peter and All Hallow's Catholic Church,
Sacramento, California, USA.

*****

Printed by:
Floreat Systems
Catholic Archdiocese of Benin Printing Press
30, Airport Road,
Benin City, Edo State, Nigeria
08133967455

We dedicate this book

to

Lisa's late mum,

Maggie Simmons

and

to all legionaries

of Mary.

FOREWORD

In the message of the angel to Mary in Luke 1:30: *Mary; you have found favour with God,* Mary is being described as 'kecharitomene,' that is, one who is highly favoured. Mary received the favour of God for herself and for all God's children.

To this end, the story of the drama of salvation will remain incomplete without considering the singular and wilful obedience of Mary to the message of the angel regarding the birth of the Son of God, Jesus Christ. The impactful 'yes' of Mary to the will of God has changed the relational dynamic between God and humankind, as she now helps everyone within her motherly care to say a similar 'yes' to God.

In the spirit of accepting the will of God and finding meaning, direction and purpose in life, Fr. Emmanuel Okami and Lisa Timms have, in this book, *'In the Arms of Mary,'* provided a roadmap to help Catholics and Christians of similar religious persuasion to navigate the rigours of life through the lens of the Blessed Virgin Mary. With depth of insight and clarity of vision, the authors have presented succinct and spiritually edifying reflections by using the tools of Scripture and tradition to explore and explain how being 'in the arms of Mary' can help us to also participate and share in the favour of God which Mary received in full.

These thirty-one days of reflection will help all devotees of the Blessed Virgin Mary and any interested person to embrace authentic Christian living by meditating on the sorrows and joys of Mary. This book is written to assist anyone who wishes to embark on a journey of spiritual orientation and re-orientation.

Fr. Moses Oluwaseun Ikuelogbon
Diocese of Buffalo, New York, USA.

★★★★★

AUTHORS' NOTE

In article 1746 of the Divine Mercy Diary, St. Faustina wrote: "To give worthy praise to the Lord's mercy, we unite ourselves with Your Immaculate Mother, for then our hymn will be more pleasing to You because She is chosen from among men and angels. Through Her, as through a pure crystal, Your mercy was passed on to us. Through Her, man became pleasing to God; Through Her, streams of grace flowed down upon us."

If we allow the Holy Spirit to guide our reflection on the history of our salvation, we cannot but marvel at the role that our Blessed Mother played. The Blessed Virgin Mary should be the heroine of everyone who understands the mystery of human redemption. She was the woman chosen and carefully prepared by God to be the means through which God the Father, through the power of the Holy Spirit, gave the world His greatest gift- His only begotten Son.

Our Mother Mary is worthy not just of simple admiration but of great honour.

God in His goodness has also ordained that she should not just be a help in ages past but an ever-present help to all who will have recourse to her at any and every age and time.

Any spirituality that doesn't accommodate the ever-glorious mother of Jesus is suspicious and troubling. More so, with all her apparitions and the testimonies of her powerful intercession, it should be worrisome that some people have yet to embrace this source of grace, this channel of blessing, this cause of joy that God has given to humankind.

The only conceivable cause of some people's rejection of Mary is that the evil one has blindfolded them. We are grateful to God that we are among those blessed to come to the knowledge of this saving truth.

We also clearly recognise that it is our bounden duty to proclaim to the world that there is the hope of graces and fountain of blessing available through Mary, made possible by her Son's merit. Everyone deserves to benefit from her maternal help, and we all have a mandate to work towards this.

Through this book, *In the Arms of Mary, Thirty-One Days with Our Blessed Mother*, we hope to bring about this awareness and a deepening of devotion to Our Lady. This book is meant to help us to walk more closely with Jesus, being carried in the arms of Mary. It is arranged in such a way that each day is accompanied by a careful study of the Word of God, a reflection and prayers.

The aim of this is not just to reflect on the example of Our Lady's heroic life or to merely seek an intercession without any willingness to accept her as a loving mother; the grand aim of this book is to invite and challenge us to deepen our intimacy with the Blessed Mother of our Redeemer, knowing full well that she is a sure help to all who have recourse to her.

It is, therefore, our prayer that this book will help someone to love Mary more, have recourse to her more fervently, deepen their relationship with her and one day come to see her face to face in the kingdom of God where she reigns as Queen together with her Son who is King for all ages.

May everyone who reads this book, who meditates on the content and faithfully says the prayers, obtain through our Mother, temporal help in this world, mercy at the hour of their death and the gift of eternal salvation when the curtain of life closes.

Humbly yours,

Fr. Emmanuel Okami
&
Lisa Timms

★★★★★

REVIEWS

This book is simply beautiful! *In the Arms of Mary*, by Fr. Emmanuel Okami and Lisa Timms has taken me on a thirty-one-day journey of life illumination through the pathway of Mother Mary, from the time of the Annunciation.

Mary said yes to the Divine will and she remains the handmaid of the Lord who leads us towards God.

After being taken up into heaven, Mary did not distance herself from us but continues to be even closer to us, shining her light in our lives. We all need her help and comfort to face the trials and challenges of daily life. We need to feel that she is our mother in the concrete situations of our lives.

In this book, reflections based on titles and invocations of Mary, take us through a journey of faith destined to guide us and give us strength on the path that leads us to the creator of heaven and earth. This book makes me fall in LOVE with Mary even more deeply. As they have with me, may these reflections lift you to greater heights of faith, and may you discover the great love that our Most Holy Mother has for you. Above all, may you discover that it is only in turning over your life entirely to God, that you will know the greatest possible joy.

Through Mary, let this book guide you as she points us to her Son, Jesus. He gave us His mother, to be ours, so that in times of difficulty we may always count on her by simply asking her to take over.

One must remain in prayer with Mary, the mother given to us by Christ from the cross. May she help us with her motherly care to follow Jesus, to know the truth and to live in love.

Catherine Waweru
Parishioner of Holy Redeemer Catholic Church, Wexham, UK.

★★★★★

Reading *In the Arms of Mary* by Fr. Emmanuel Okami and Lisa Timms, has brought me even closer to our Blessed Lady. The reflections of each day are an inspiration and truly God sent. Our Mother's love is deeply rooted in our Catholic lives. She prays for us and intercedes for us always. She walked through life before us and therefore understands our daily dilemmas.

Reading this book reminds us that Our Lady feels our daily pains and struggles and understands us. She is ready and always at hand to pray for us. She is our stronghold and covers us with her mantle. My prayer is that this book touches whoever reads it, in the same way that it touched and transformed me in my daily life. Enjoy reading and remain blessed.

Mrs Joyce Waithera Mburu
St. Gedd's Catholic Church, Ilford, UK.

★★★★★

In this insightful book of reflections, *In the Arms of Mary* by Fr. Emmanuel Okami and Lisa Timms, Mary is once again presented to us as a daily companion worthy of taking us through the journey of life with her experience and prayers. The authors of this write up creatively reveal the depth of love and care a soul can enjoy in the warm embrace of the Blessed Virgin Mary, who promised succour to all who believe in her perpetual mediation before the throne of Grace.

The right steps or ways to journey with Our Lady and to seek her maternal help for a period of 31 good days in this work are clearly outlined by the authors in a tripartite form of reflections and prayers from the Scriptures, the titles and invocations of the Blessed Virgin Mary and the enduring teachings of the Church as taught in the dogmas of the Blessed Virgin Mary.

This book is suitable for all Christians who wish to enrol themselves in the spiritual 'School' of the Blessed Virgin Mary in order to grow in virtue and also to live a life worthy of their calling, just as Mary did.

Rev. Fr. James Taiye Ipinlaye
Administrator Archangels Catholic School,
Ilorin Diocese, Nigeria.

★★★★★

IN THE ARMS OF
MARY

Thirty-One Days with Our Blessed Mother

Fr. Emmanuel Okami & Lisa Timms

TABLE OF CONTENTS

*REFLECTIONS BASED ON THE GOSPEL NARRATIVES
AND ACTS OF THE APOSTLES*

REFLECTIONS BASED ON TITLES AND INVOCATIONS OF MARY

REFLECTIONS BASED ON THE CHURCH'S TEACHINGS AND DOGMA ON MARY

PRAYERS IN HONOUR OF OUR LADY

HYMNS IN HONOUR OF THE BLESSED VIRGIN

★★★★★

Happy, indeed sublimely happy, is the person to whom the Holy Spirit reveals the secret of Mary, thus imparting to him true knowledge of her. Happy the person to whom the Holy Spirit opens this enclosed garden for him to enter, and to whom the Holy Spirit gives access to this sealed fountain where he can draw water and drink deep draughts of the living waters of grace. That person will find only grace and no creature in the most lovable Virgin Mary. But he will find that the infinitely holy and exalted God is at the same time infinitely solicitous for him and understands his weaknesses. Since God is everywhere, he can be found everywhere, even in hell. But there is no place where God can be more present to his creature and more sympathetic to human weakness than in Mary. It was indeed for this very purpose that he came down from heaven. Everywhere else he is the Bread of the strong and the Bread of angels but living in Mary he is the Bread of children.

The Secret of Mary,
by **Saint Louis Marie de Montfort**

★★★★★

REFLECTIONS BASED ON THE GOSPEL NARRATIVES AND ACTS OF THE APOSTLES

DAY 1

MARY SURRENDERED TO GOD'S WILL

26 In the sixth month the Angel Gabriel was sent from God to a city of Galilee named Nazareth, 27 to a virgin betrothed to a man whose name was Joseph, of the house of David; and the virgin's name was Mary. 28 And he came to her and said, "Hail, O favoured one, the Lord is with you!"
29 But she was greatly troubled at the saying and considered in her mind what sort of greeting this might be. 30 And the angel said to her, "Do not be afraid, Mary, for you have found favour with God. 31 And behold, you will conceive in your womb and bear a son, and you shall call His name Jesus.

32 He will be great and will be called the Son of the Most High; and the Lord God will give to Him the throne of His father David, 33 and He will reign over the house of Jacob forever; and of His kingdom there will be no end." 34 And Mary said to the angel, "How shall this be, since I have no husband?"

35 And the angel said to her, "The Holy Spirit will come upon you, and the power of the Most High will overshadow you; therefore the child to be born will be called holy, the Son of God. 36 And behold, your kinswoman Elizabeth in her old age has also conceived a son; and this is the sixth month with her who was called barren. 37 For with God nothing will be impossible."

38 And Mary said, "Behold, I am the handmaid of the Lord; let it be to me according to your word." And the angel departed from her.

LUKE 1:26-38

Reflection

The Angel Gabriel was sent to announce to the Blessed Virgin Mary, the eternal plan of the Father and Mary's role in that plan. Even without fully understanding, Mary accepted to cooperate with God's plan. She was very clear on her identity; she was the handmaid of God. She surrendered the greatest gift she had to God, her will. By that simple statement, Mary confessed that she belonged wholly and entirely to the Lord and what the Lord wanted was all that mattered to her.

Beloved children of God, like Mary, are you willing to surrender your will to the Lord? Are you ready to embrace God's plans for your life, even when it is different from what you had planned and anticipated? Are you willing to allow God to use you for His purpose in any way He might choose?

As you come to the Lord in prayer, are you bent on what you want or what He might will for you? Sometimes accepting God's will can be very difficult but it is in accepting God's will that we find peace and we live our lives to the full.

Prayer
O Mother of my Saviour, intercede for me to your Son, that by the help of the Holy Spirit, I may surrender my will, desire and plans and embrace courageously God's will for my life.
Amen.

Hail Holy Queen
Hail, Holy Queen, Mother of Mercy,
Hail our life, our sweetness and our hope.
To thee do we cry, O poor banished children of Eve.
To thee do we send up our sighs, mourning and weeping in this vale of tears.
Turn then, most gracious advocate, thine eyes of mercy towards us,
and after this exile, show unto us the blessed fruit of thy womb, Jesus.

O clement, O loving, O sweet Virgin Mary.

Intention

For those finding it difficult to accept God's will in their lives at this moment, and those struggling with their faith, we pray that our Mother Mary may intercede for them and obtain for them the grace of courageous resignation to God's will.

Pray

One Our Father, one Hail Mary, one Glory be.

★★★★★

DAY 2

MARY TRUSTED IN THE LORD TO SORT HER OUT

18 Now the birth of Jesus the Messiah took place in this way. When His mother Mary had been engaged to Joseph, but before they lived together, she was found to be with child from the Holy Spirit. 19 Her husband Joseph, being a righteous man and unwilling to expose her to public disgrace, planned to dismiss her quietly. 20 But just when he had resolved to do this, an angel of the Lord appeared to him in a dream and said, "Joseph, son of David, do not be afraid to take Mary as your wife, for the child conceived in her is from the Holy Spirit. 21 She will bear a son, and you are to name Him Jesus, for He will save His people from their sins." 22 All this took place to fulfil what had been spoken by the Lord through the prophet: **23** *"Look, the virgin shall conceive and bear a son, and they shall name Him Emmanuel," which means, "God is with us."* **24** *When Joseph awoke from sleep, he did as the angel of the Lord commanded him; he took her as his wife,* **25** *but had no marital relations with her until she had borne a son; and he named Him Jesus.*

MATTHEW 1:18-25

Reflection

After accepting the message of the Angel Gabriel, the natural worry of Mary ought to have been "who will tell Joseph, how will I explain to him?"

However, Mary trusted in the Lord to sort out everything in His own way and God did sort it out. God spoke to Joseph in a dream. He explained everything to Joseph and the situation was miraculously resolved. Mary only had to trust, and God worked in a way she never could have imagined.

The calmness of Mary in the midst of this confusing situation is a big lesson for us. She was a woman who was calm in a stormy situation. She did not give in to worry, distress or anxiety. She allowed the Lord to sort things out. For her, if God was responsible for her situation, God would take care of her and all that concerned her.

Dear children of God, let us learn from Mary to be calm and surrender every situation to the Lord to sort out. God cannot put us in a situation and abandon us.

He cannot send us on a difficult voyage and remain indifferent to our plight. This was the faith of Mary, and this is what God expects from us.

Prayer
Holy Mother of my Redeemer, obtain for me true serenity. Help me to face every stormy situation with confidence that God is always in control and He will sort things out the best way.
Amen.

Hail Holy Queen
Hail, Holy Queen, Mother of Mercy,
Hail our life, our sweetness and our hope.
To thee do we cry, O poor banished children of Eve.
To thee do we send up our sighs, mourning and weeping in this vale of tears.
Turn then, most gracious advocate, thine eyes of mercy towards us, and after this exile, show unto us the blessed fruit of thy womb, Jesus.
O clement, O loving, O sweet Virgin Mary.

Intention
Let us pray for those having marriage and family challenges. May they rejoice to receive the maternal help of our Blessed Mother.

Pray
One Our Father, one Hail Mary, one Glory be.

*****

DAY 3

MARY VISITED ELIZABETH

39 In those days Mary set out and went with haste to a Judean town in the hill country, 40 where she entered the house of Zechariah and greeted Elizabeth.

LUKE 1:39-40

Reflection
As soon as Mary received the news about the wonder of God in the life of Elizabeth, she hastened to rejoice with her, to support her in her present state and to share her own experience with Elizabeth.

By this visitation, Mary demonstrated great charity and sensitivity. She sensed the need of Elizabeth and was willing to go and help her.

How sensitive am I to the needs of those around me? How selfless am I in my dealing with others? Am I willing to sacrifice my time, resources and plans to be there for others in their needs? Am I so comfortable with and in myself that I do not want to be bothered by the needs and challenges of others?

Mary reminds us of the need to be there for others in their needs, to support, comfort, counsel, encourage and give a helping hand even when we ourselves are having our own personal struggles.

Prayer
O Mother of Charity, help me to be charitable as you are. May the Holy Spirit open my eyes to the needs of others, and may I be willing to support them in any way I can.
Amen.

Hail Holy Queen
Hail, Holy Queen, Mother of Mercy,
Hail our life, our sweetness and our hope.
To thee do we cry, O poor banished children of Eve.
To thee do we send up our sighs, mourning and weeping in this vale of tears.

Turn then, most gracious advocate, thine eyes of mercy towards us,
and after this exile, show unto us the blessed fruit of thy womb, Jesus.
O clement, O loving, O sweet Virgin Mary.

Intention
Let us pray today for those who are lonely, feeling unloved or abandoned. May they experience the consolation of God's love in their lives and may God use us to bring them comfort and joy.

Pray
One Our Father, one Hail Mary, one Glory be.

DAY 4

MARY IS BLESSED AMONG ALL WOMEN

42 Elizabeth exclaimed with a loud cry, "Blessed are you among women, and blessed is the fruit of your womb. 43 And why has this happened to me, that the mother of my Lord comes to me?

LUKE 1:42-43

Reflection
Elizabeth exclaimed with a loud cry, "Blessed are you among women." Yes, Mary is indeed 'blessed' among all women. She was chosen from all eternity to be the Mother of God the Son, who is the Saviour of the

world. Mary is blessed as a chosen vessel. She is blessed for accepting God's will, and she is blessed for cooperating with God.

Like Mary, we are also blessed people. God has chosen us in Christ Jesus. He has redeemed us and called us into His kingdom of light. We have received the gift of His Spirit and been called to become members of His Holy people.

How grateful am I for the privileges I have received? How faithful am I to the one who has called, sanctified, justified and glorified Himself in me? Do I live my life joyfully as someone blessed and honoured by God, or do I allow misery, ingratitude and sin to deprive me of the joy of my salvation?

Prayer
O Blessed Mother of my Redeemer, as I glorify God for His graces and blessings upon you, I rejoice in the graces and blessings I have received likewise. I declare that I am blessed, and I shall be a source of blessing to others.
Amen.

Hail Holy Queen
Hail, Holy Queen, Mother of Mercy,
Hail our life, our sweetness and our hope.
To thee do we cry, O poor banished children of Eve.

To thee do we send up our sighs, mourning and weeping in this vale of tears.

Turn then, most gracious advocate, thine eyes of mercy towards us,

and after this exile, show unto us the blessed fruit of thy womb, Jesus.

O clement, O loving, O sweet Virgin Mary.

Intention

Let us pray for those who do not honour our Mother Mary. May they come to know the truth and have recourse to her as a sure help and hope of the human race.

Pray

One Our Father, one Hail Mary, one Glory be.

DAY 5

THE PRESENCE OF MARY

43 And why has this happened to me, that the mother of my Lord comes to me? 44 For as soon as I heard the sound of your greeting, the child in my womb leaped for joy.

LUKE 1:43-44

Reflection

Elizabeth confessed that as soon as she heard the greetings of Mary, something happened to her; the child in her womb leapt for joy. The presence of Mary brought joy not just to Elizabeth but also to the child in her womb.

Many people today are living in the morass of bitterness; wallowing and wasting away in a life of sorrow and misery.

Like Mary, we are called to be ministers of joy, harbingers of happiness; we are called to spread the joy of the Lord. We cannot spread what has not taken root in us, and as such, we are first called to be people of joy.

This is a joy that comes from the assurance that we are loved by God, and we are special to Him. He is looking after us, there is hope for us in Him. His plans for us are good and we are living not according to chance but His wise providence. This is a joy that comes from our reflection on the mystery of our salvation.

This joy is not based on what we possess but who we possess. It is a joy that is not deflected by suffering or deflated by circumstances but is a joy that the Holy Spirit causes in a soul.

With this torrent of joy, we can go out and sow the seed of joy in the lives of others, reassuring them that when God is involved, life can be a drama of grace and happiness.

Prayer
O Mother of Joy, your visit to Elizabeth brought her great joy. By the power of the Holy Spirit, may joy

well up within me and be communicated to all those
I may come in contact with.
Amen.

Hail Holy Queen

Hail, Holy Queen, Mother of Mercy,
Hail our life, our sweetness and our hope.
To thee do we cry, O poor banished children of Eve.
To thee do we send up our sighs, mourning and
weeping in this vale of tears.
Turn then, most gracious advocate, thine eyes of
mercy towards us,
and after this exile, show unto us the blessed fruit of
thy womb, Jesus.
O clement, O loving, O sweet Virgin Mary.

Intention

Let us pray for all those who are depressed, bitter,
sorrowful and unhappy. May the Holy Spirit fill
them with His joy.

Pray

One Our Father, one Hail Mary, one Glory be.

★★★★★

DAY 6

BLESSED IS SHE WHO BELIEVES

45 And blessed is she who believed that there would be a fulfilment of what was spoken to her by the Lord.

LUKE 1:45

Reflection
Elizabeth told Mary, *blessed is she who believed that there would be a fulfilment of what was spoken to her by the Lord.*

This powerful statement of Elizabeth to Mary is an eternal truth; blessed indeed is anyone who believes in the message of the Lord.

We are truly blessed if we believe what the Lord has promised through His Word. We are blessed when we believe what the Lord is teaching through His Church, and we are blessed when we receive with faith, the message of our Blessed Mother made known to us through her many apparitions. We are blessed if we believe in the power, goodness, love, mercy and plans of God for us.

Do you believe in the promises of God, especially in the dark days of your life? Do you believe that you can trust God and He won't disappoint you? Do you believe in what the Word of God says and all that the Church proclaims as the truth?

Prayer
O Blessed Mother, even without fully under-standing, you accepted the message of the angel and you believed in what had been announced to you. Help me to believe in the promises of God for my life and help me to faithfully uphold all that the Church teaches as saving truth.
Amen.

Hail Holy Queen
Hail, Holy Queen, Mother of Mercy,
Hail our life, our sweetness and our hope.
To thee do we cry, O poor banished children of Eve.
To thee do we send up our sighs, mourning and weeping in this vale of tears.

Turn then, most gracious advocate, thine eyes of mercy towards us, and after this exile, show unto us the blessed fruit of thy womb, Jesus.

O clement, O loving, O sweet Virgin Mary.

Intention

Let us pray for sceptics within the community of faith; those who are members of the body of Christ but do not believe in what the Church teaches. May the light of faith dispel the darkness of unbelief.

Pray

One Our Father, one Hail Mary, one Glory be.

DAY 7

MARY THE GOD-BEARER (THEOTOKOS)

30 The angel said to her, "Do not be afraid, Mary, for you have found favour with God. 31 And now, you will conceive in your womb and bear a son, and you will name Him Jesus. 32 He will be great and will be called the Son of the Most High, and the Lord God will give to Him the throne of His ancestor David. 33 He will reign over the house of Jacob forever, and of His kingdom there will be no end."

LUKE 1:30-33

Reflection

Mary is addressed as the new Ark of the Covenant because she bore within her womb what the Old Testament Ark of the Covenant foreshadows.

In her womb, she bore God the Son and she took Him wherever she went. She gave flesh to the Divine Son and that is why it is impossible to separate the Body of Jesus from that of Mary, because it was in her that the Divine Son took His flesh.

Mary is properly addressed as 'Theotokos', meaning God-bearer. As Christians, we are called in our own way to be God-bearers; to carry the love, presence and power of God wherever we go.

God-in-us must reflect in everything we do, anyone we meet, any place we go. Everyone who encounters us must feel something of the presence of God and His glory.

Do I allow God's presence to be visible to others through me? Do people experience something of God's presence, love and power when they meet me? Created in the image and likeness of God, do I allow God's image and likeness to be conspicuous in my life?

Prayer

Holy Mary, Ark of the New Covenant and God-bearer, help me to be a bearer of God's glory, image, likeness and presence wherever I may find myself, so that through me, others may come to experience the awesomeness of God.

Amen.

Hail Holy Queen

Hail, Holy Queen, Mother of Mercy,

Hail our life, our sweetness and our hope.

To thee do we cry, O poor banished children of Eve.

To thee do we send up our sighs, mourning and weeping in this vale of tears.

Turn then, most gracious advocate, thine eyes of mercy towards us, and after this exile, show unto us the blessed fruit of thy womb, Jesus.

O clement, O loving, O sweet Virgin Mary.

Intention

Let us pray for those who are ashamed and afraid to witness to their faith, and for those persecuted on account of their faith. May the Holy Spirit come alive anew in them with greater courage, fervent spirit and holy zeal.

Pray

One Our Father, one Hail Mary, one Glory be.

★★★★★

DAY 8

MY SOUL MAGNIFIES THE LORD

46 And Mary said, "My soul magnifies the Lord, 47 and my spirit rejoices in God my Saviour."

LUKE 1:46-47

Reflection
Following the praises showered on Mary by her kinswoman Elizabeth, Mary returned all the glory and honour to God. She exclaimed: *My soul magnifies the Lord...*

In other words, "all glory and praise belong to the Lord. Only God is worthy of all my praises; nothing in me justifies this honour. I direct the acknowledgement to the source of all that is good in me. I praise Him not just with my lips but the depth of my soul. I recognise His hands at work, and I exalt Him."

This statement of Mary should not depart from our lips whether in joy or sorrow, in need or abundance. Let us learn to say, "My soul magnifies the Lord."

Dear friends, do you realise that everything good and beautiful in you comes from God and that to Him belongs all the glory in your life? Do you often keep in mind that God must always be magnified and exalted above all else, above every person, above every situation and challenge?

Prayer
Mother of love, teach me to magnify the Lord always and every time. Let me respond to every situation, whether pleasant or otherwise, by saying, "My soul magnifies the Lord."
Amen.

Hail Holy Queen
Hail, Holy Queen, Mother of Mercy,
Hail our life, our sweetness and our hope.
To thee do we cry, O poor banished children of Eve.
To thee do we send up our sighs, mourning and weeping in this vale of tears.
Turn then, most gracious advocate, thine eyes of mercy towards us,

and after this exile, show unto us the blessed fruit of thy womb, Jesus.

O clement, O loving, O sweet Virgin Mary.

Intention

For those who are depressed, sad and bitter, may the Lord manifest His healing love and power in their lives, so that their souls may rejoice in the Lord.

Pray

One Our Father, one Hail Mary, one Glory be.

★★★★★

DAY 9

MARY GAVE BIRTH TO JESUS IN A MANGER

1 In those days a decree went out from Emperor Augustus that all the world should be registered. 2 This was the first registration and was taken while Quirinius was governor of Syria. 3 All went to their own towns to be registered. 4 Joseph also went from the town of Nazareth in Galilee to Judea, to the city of David called Bethlehem, because he was descended from the house and family of David. 5 He went to be registered with Mary, to whom he was engaged and who was expecting a child. 6 While they were there, the time came for her to deliver her child. 7 And she gave birth to her firstborn son and wrapped Him in bands of cloth, and laid Him in a manger, because there was no place for them in the inn.

LUKE 2:1-7

Reflection

When the time came for Mary to be delivered of her child, there was no room for them in the inn, so she gave birth to Jesus in a stable. Mary gave birth and laid the Creator of the whole world in a manger. There is a deep mystery and great wisdom in the fact that Jesus was born and laid in a manger. Is it not appropriate that the Good Shepherd should be given birth to where animals are kept? God gave humanity a paradise, we turned it into a manger. God sent a Saviour who was to restore humanity back to paradise and so He was laid in a manger. This is the wisdom of God at work.

Mary accepted to be delivered of her child in a manger. This testifies to her humility and simplicity. Dear children of God, let us ask ourselves - how humble are we? How detached are we from the vanities of life? Do we really set more value on the things of heaven than on the things of this world?

May we learn from Mary to be humble, simple and grateful, no matter the condition.

Prayer

Our Queen O Mary, you gave birth to the Saviour in a manger. Teach me to learn how to live a life of

simplicity, be poor in spirit and to focus on what truly matters in life.
Amen.

Hail Holy Queen
Hail, Holy Queen, Mother of Mercy,
Hail our life, our sweetness and our hope.
To thee do we cry, O poor banished children of Eve.
To thee do we send up our sighs, mourning and weeping in this vale of tears.
Turn then, most gracious advocate, thine eyes of mercy towards us,
and after this exile, show unto us the blessed fruit of thy womb, Jesus.
O clement, O loving, O sweet Virgin Mary.

Intention
Let us pray for all who are pregnant, that the Lord through Our Lady's intercession, may grant them a safe delivery.

Pray
One Our Father, one Hail Mary, one Glory be.

★★★★★

DAY 10

MARY AND JOSEPH PRESENTED JESUS

22 When the time came for their purification according to the law of Moses, they brought Him up to Jerusalem to present Him to the Lord 23 (as it is written in the law of the Lord, "Every firstborn male shall be designated as holy to the Lord"), 24 and they offered a sacrifice according to what is stated in the law of the Lord, "a pair of turtledoves or two young pigeons."

LUKE 2:22-24

Reflection

The parents of Jesus presented Him at the temple when the time came for their purification. Here, the parents of Jesus are presented to us as devout Jews who faithfully observed the Jewish laws and ordinances. They did all that the law required for Jesus.

Let us reflect on the faithfulness of Mary and Joseph, and their conscientious practice of the requirements of the law, which expressed their love for God and respect for religion.

Let us ask ourselves, how faithful am I to the laws of the Church? Do I joyfully fulfil my religious obligations? Do I faithfully follow the practices of the Church and respect her observances? Do I keep the day of the Lord holy by going for Mass and resting from servile works? Do I contribute to the support of God's ministers and the Church? Do I make good and regular confessions? Do I receive Communion with proper preparation regularly? Do I fast on the days approved by the Church? Do I respect the Church's teaching on marriage and family life? Do I understand, believe and teach accurately what the Church professes?

Prayer
O Mary, you are the Mother of the Church and a faithful observer of the law of God. Obtain for me something of your faith, obedience and devotion. Amen.

Hail Holy Queen
Hail, Holy Queen, Mother of Mercy,
Hail our life, our sweetness and our hope.
To thee do we cry, O poor banished children of Eve.
To thee do we send up our sighs, mourning and weeping in this vale of tears.
Turn then, most gracious advocate, thine eyes of mercy towards us,
and after this exile, show unto us the blessed fruit of thy womb, Jesus.
O clement, O loving, O sweet Virgin Mary.

Intention
Let us pray for all those who oppose the Church and her teaching. May the Spirit of truth rest upon them for enlightenment and conversion.

Pray
One Our Father, one Hail Mary, one Glory be.

★★★★★

DAY 11

THE PROPHECY OF SIMEON

28 Simeon took Him in his arms and praised God, saying, 29 "Master, now you are dismissing your servant in peace, according to your Word; 30 for my eyes have seen your salvation, 31 which you have prepared in the presence of all peoples, 32 a light for revelation to the Gentiles and for glory to your people Israel." 33 And the child's father and mother were amazed at what was being said about Him. 34 Then Simeon blessed them and said to His mother Mary, "This child is destined for the falling and the rising of many in Israel, and to be a sign that will be opposed 35 so that the inner thoughts of many will be revealed—and a sword will pierce your own soul too." LUKE 2:28-35

Reflection

Simeon took the child Jesus in his arms; he blessed God for the child and, turning to our Blessed Mother, he prophesied that her child was destined for the fall and rising of many and that a sword would pierce her soul too. This must have filled Mary with sorrow; it is not the type of prophecy we want to hear about a new child. None of us wants a sword to pierce our soul. We do not rejoice to expect agony.

However, Mary accepted this prophecy trusting in God and accepting that God's plan is always for our good.

Dear Children of God, what is your response when you hear or receive a report or message that is unsettling? Do you have confidence in God and trust in His love and good purpose, or do you become angry, aggressive, complaining to God and bitter to others?

Prayer

Mary our Blessed Mother, you accepted with courage, calmness and peace, the troubling prophecy of Simeon that a sword would pierce your soul too. Help me to accept with equal courage the cross I am called to bear in my Christian journey.
Amen.

Hail Holy Queen

Hail, Holy Queen, Mother of Mercy,
Hail our life, our sweetness and our hope.
To thee do we cry, O poor banished children of Eve.
To thee do we send up our sighs, mourning and weeping in this vale of tears.
Turn then, most gracious advocate, thine eyes of mercy towards us,
and after this exile, show unto us the blessed fruit of thy womb, Jesus.
O clement, O loving, O sweet Virgin Mary.

Intention

Let us pray for all those who have received unpleasant reports about their health, family or job, that they may learn to trust in God's good plans for their lives.

Pray

One Our Father, one Hail Mary, one Glory be.

★★★★★

DAY 12

MARY PONDERED ON GOD'S MESSAGE

15 When the angels went away from them into heaven, the shepherds said to one another, "Let us go over to Bethlehem and see this thing that has happened, which the Lord has made known to us." 16 And they went with haste, and found Mary and Joseph, and the babe lying in a manger. 17 And when they saw it, they made known the saying which had been told to them concerning this child; 18 and all who heard it wondered at what the shepherds told them. 19 But Mary kept all these things, pondering them in her heart. 20 And the shepherds returned, glorifying and praising God for all they had heard and seen, as it had been told them.

LUKE 2:15-20

Reflection

Mary heard the message of the shepherds and pondered this in her heart. Again in Luke 2:51, after finding Jesus in the temple, Mary kept in her heart all that had happened and what Jesus had told them.

Mary becomes for us a model of how we can profit from the Word of God. We need to not just hear or read God's Word, but we must spend time pondering on the meaning of the message of truth and the practical application. We must seek to grow in our knowledge and appreciation of the Word of God.

Let us ask ourselves, how often do I read the Word of God? How often do I ponder further on the texts I have read or the homilies I have heard? Do I consciously seek to apply the Word of God to my daily life? Do I allow the Word of God to influence my words, thoughts and actions and to bear fruit in me?

Prayer

O Mother of the incarnate Word, help me to treasure in my heart the word of grace I hear daily. Through the help of the Holy Spirit, may I desire to study the Word of God and grow in my understanding of it. Amen.

Hail Holy Queen

Hail, Holy Queen, Mother of Mercy,

Hail our life, our sweetness and our hope.

To thee do we cry, O poor banished children of Eve.

To thee do we send up our sighs, mourning and weeping in this vale of tears.

Turn then, most gracious advocate, thine eyes of mercy towards us,

and after this exile, show unto us the blessed fruit of thy womb, Jesus.

O clement, O loving, O sweet Virgin Mary.

Intention

For those who do not believe in God, for those who have lost the faith in which they were baptised, may the light of grace dispel the darkness of unbelief from their lives.

Pray

One Our Father, one Hail Mary, one Glory be.

DAY 13

MARY AND JOSEPH ESCAPED WITH JESUS TO EGYPT

13 Now after they had left, an angel of the Lord appeared to Joseph in a dream and said, "Get up, take the child and His mother, and flee to Egypt, and remain there until I tell you; for Herod is about to search for the child, to destroy Him." 14 Then Joseph got up, took the child and His mother by night, and went to Egypt, 15 and remained there until the death of Herod. This was to fulfil what had been spoken by the Lord through the prophet, "Out of Egypt I have called my Son."

MATTHEW 2:13-15

Reflection

Herod, the wicked king, resolutely sought to kill the child Jesus. As a result of this, Mary and Joseph had to run away to faraway Egypt.

As I read the account of this incident, I wondered in my mind, "if this child is the Son of the Most High, why can't the Most High stop Herod? Why did the Holy Family need to run? Why should they go through this stress to protect the Child of God?"

Interestingly, the flight to Egypt was part of God's plan. Jesus in Egypt calls to mind His role as a Saviour. Just as Moses led God's people from slavery in Egypt, this child will ultimately lead humanity from slavery of sin to true and lasting freedom.

Mary and Joseph did not complain because of what they had to undergo; they accepted it in good faith, in total resignation to the will of God who is infinitely perfect.

Dear children of God, how often do I complain about what challenges I have to endure in my life? How often do I blame God for not saving me from a particular stress, tension or struggle? How often do I blame God for the cross He wants me to carry? How often do I challenge His love and goodness?

May we learn from Mary to be calm and be more trusting and to see God present in both the glorious and the sorrowful mysteries of our lives.

Prayer

O Mother of my Saviour, you underwent great suffering and difficulties to protect the baby Jesus from Herod and yet you didn't complain. Help me to bear my crosses of life without complaint, and to accept my challenges with greater faith and courage. Amen.

Hail Holy Queen

Hail, Holy Queen, Mother of Mercy,
Hail our life, our sweetness and our hope.
To thee do we cry, O poor banished children of Eve.
To thee do we send up our sighs, mourning and weeping in this vale of tears.
Turn then, most gracious advocate, thine eyes of mercy towards us, and after this exile, show unto us the blessed fruit of thy womb, Jesus.
O clement, O loving, O sweet Virgin Mary.

Intention

Let us pray for those exiled, for refugees, for fugitives, for those driven from their homelands. May the Lord be gracious to them and cause His face to shine upon them.

Pray

One Our Father, one Hail Mary, one Glory be.

★★★★★

DAY 14

THE FINDING IN THE TEMPLE

41 Now every year His parents went to Jerusalem for the festival of the Passover. 42 And when He was twelve years old, they went up as usual for the festival. 43 When the festival was ended and they started to return, the boy Jesus stayed behind in Jerusalem, but His parents did not know it. 44 Assuming that He was in the group of travellers, they went a day's journey. Then they started to look for Him among their relatives and friends. 45 When they did not find Him, they returned to Jerusalem to search for Him. 46 After three days they found Him in the temple, sitting among the teachers, listening to them and asking them questions. 47 And all who heard Him were amazed at His understanding and

*His answers. **48** When His parents saw Him they were astonished; and His mother said to Him, "Child, why have you treated us like this? Look, your father and I have been searching for you in great anxiety." **49** He said to them, "Why were you searching for me? Did you not know that I must be in my Father's house?" **50** But they did not understand what He said to them. **51** Then He went down with them and came to Nazareth and was obedient to them. His mother treasured all these things in her heart.*

LUKE 2:41-51

Reflection

The parents of Jesus took Him to the temple in Jerusalem for the feast of the Passover. They left thinking He was with their relatives, and when they could not find Him, they searched for three days. Eventually they found Him in the temple listening to the elders and asking them questions.

Let us imagine the pains and sorrows of our Blessed Mother losing her only child. Let us imagine her restlessness and sleepless nights, her loss of appetite and the sadness that must have engulfed her spirit.

Think of the joy in her heart when she found Jesus, how grateful she was to God, even when Jesus responded that they shouldn't have worried about Him because He was doing His father's business. Far from being angry, Mary took these words to heart and then took Jesus back with them to Nazareth.

Like Mary, does it bother me if I am separated from Jesus? Do I dread not being able to come before Jesus in adoration or being able to receive Him in Holy Communion? Do I fear being separated from His love by sin? Do I dread being separated from Him in eternity?

Prayer
O my Dearest Mother, you knew no peace, you had no rest until you found your missing Son. Intercede for me, your unworthy child, so that I may never be separated from your worthy Son, in time or eternity. Amen.

Hail Holy Queen
Hail, Holy Queen, Mother of Mercy,
Hail our life, our sweetness and our hope.
To thee do we cry, O poor banished children of Eve.
To thee do we send up our sighs, mourning and weeping in this vale of tears.
Turn then, most gracious advocate, thine eyes of mercy towards us,
and after this exile, show unto us the blessed fruit of thy womb, Jesus.
O clement, O loving, O sweet Virgin Mary.

Intention
Let us pray for those searching for their missing loved ones. Mother Mary, come to their aid and may they

be happily reunited with those they love but they have not heard from.

Pray
One Our Father, one Hail Mary, one Glory be.

★★★★★

DAY 15

MARY'S SENSITIVITY

1 On the third day there was a wedding in Cana of Galilee, and the mother of Jesus was there. 2 Jesus and His disciples had also been invited to the wedding. 3 When the wine gave out, the mother of Jesus said to Him, "They have no wine."

JOHN 2:1-3

Reflection

At the marriage feast of Cana in Galilee, Mary sensed the trouble of the couple as they had to deal with a matter that could impact negatively on their ceremony. They had miscalculated; they had more guests than the supply of wine allowed for. In those days, wine was very important in any celebration; wine was joy, wine was life. Shortage of wine in any celebration was a bad omen for the celebrants. If people ran short of wine in a wedding ceremony, it would be seen as a pointer to the fact that the marriage would run short of joy.

You can imagine how distressed this couple were, with their hearts pounding and missing beats. The shame of not being able to feed one's guests with food was unbearable, but the embarrassment of not having enough wine was indescribable.

It was not recorded that Mary was told about this pandemonium, but she observed the situation. She went to speak with her Son. She is His mother, she knew her Son. She saw their need, their worries and confusion, and she wanted to help. She knew her Son could help, and so she went to speak to her Son. Their problem became her problem, their needs her needs. She did not want to see them embarrassed or disgraced.

Mary doesn't want any of us embarrassed or disgraced; she wishes to help us. She is a mother who is sensitive to our needs, pains and worries.

Dear Children, let us ask ourselves, how sensitive am I to the pains, needs, conditions, worries and struggles of other people? How eager am I to help people in their need? Am I sometimes indifferent, arguing that it doesn't affect or concern me? Do I claim to be unaware because I have not been sought after and begged for help?

Mary becomes an example to us, to be willing, sensitive and eager to help people in their needs. A simple action from us may save people from incalculable calamity.

Prayer
Mother of joy and hope, help me to be aware of the needs of those around me and to be eager to help and support them.
Amen.

Hail Holy Queen
Hail, Holy Queen, Mother of Mercy,
Hail our life, our sweetness and our hope.
To thee do we cry, O poor banished children of Eve.
To thee do we send up our sighs, mourning and weeping in this vale of tears.
Turn then, most gracious advocate, thine eyes of mercy towards us, and after this exile, show unto us the blessed fruit of thy womb, Jesus.
O clement, O loving, O sweet Virgin Mary.

Intention
Let us pray for those battling with suicidal thoughts as a result of their immediate challenges. May the Holy Spirit cause hope to dispel their despair.

Pray
One Our Father, one Hail Mary, one Glory be.

DAY 16

DO WHATEVER HE TELLS YOU

5 His mother said to the servants, "Do whatever He tells you."
6 Now standing there were six stone water jars for the Jewish
rites of purification, each holding twenty or thirty gallons. 7
Jesus said to them, "Fill the jars with water." And they filled
them up to the brim. 8 He said to them, "Now draw some
out, and take it to the chief steward." So they took it. 9 When
the steward tasted the water that had become wine and did
not know where it came from (though the servants who had
drawn the water knew), the steward called the bridegroom 10
and said to him, "Everyone serves the good wine first, and
then the inferior wine after the guests have become drunk. But
you have kept the good wine until now." 11 Jesus did this,

the first of His signs, in Cana of Galilee, and revealed His glory; and His disciples believed in Him.

JOHN 2:5-11

Reflection

Mary told the couple at Cana, "do whatever He tells you." She shared with them her secret. In those words, she shared with them how she had been relating with God and her Son. She simply did whatever she was told.

Mary knew that what her Son might ask of them might not make sense to them, but great things happen when we obey Jesus. What a wonderful counsel she gave them because what Jesus actually asked them to do did not appear reasonable by human logic. They had no wine, they needed wine. Cups were empty, people were thirsty for more drinks, waiters were being questioned. The steward of the feast was expectant, and then here comes this man of Galilee asking them to fill wine jars with water.

They could have protested but Mary had already told them to do whatever Jesus commanded them to do. They obeyed and shame was turned to fame, ridicule to a miracle. There was the solution to their confusion, and there was laughter, happiness and joy again, simply because they listened to Mary and did what Jesus commanded.

This is what Mary continues to teach us, she continues to remind us to do whatever Jesus asks us to do.

Dear children of God, there is a great blessing in obeying what the Lord wants us to do, but do we always obey Him, especially when what He calls us to do is different from what we had hoped or wished to do? Do we obey what Jesus has commanded us and written in the Scriptures? Are we docile and obedient to the voice of the Holy Spirit directing us to undertake and carry out tasks for the glory of God? When the Lord sends you on an assignment, journey, vocation, task, project, adventure that is different from your preferred option, will you obey? Or like Jonah, will you try to insist on your way, preference or method?

Prayer
O Mother of my Divine Master, you lived your entire life in obedience to your Son. Help me to be very obedient to Him in everything, for in obeying His commands, plans and wills for me, my life will become more meaningful and joyful.
Amen.

Hail Holy Queen
Hail, Holy Queen, Mother of Mercy,
Hail our life, our sweetness and our hope.
To thee do we cry, O poor banished children of Eve.

To thee do we send up our sighs, mourning and weeping in this vale of tears.

Turn then, most gracious advocate, thine eyes of mercy towards us,

and after this exile, show unto us the blessed fruit of thy womb, Jesus.

O clement, O loving, O sweet Virgin Mary.

Intention
Let us pray for children who are victims of broken homes, that they will know the love and care of our Blessed Mother and they will be shielded from the temptation to an evil and meaningless life.

Pray
One Our Father, one Hail Mary, one Glory be.

★★★★★

DAY 17

MARY AT THE FOOT OF THE CROSS

Meanwhile, standing near the cross of Jesus were His mother, and His mother's sister, Mary the wife of Clopas, and Mary Magdalene.

JOHN 19:25

Reflection

Our Blessed Mother followed her Son throughout His suffering, sharing in His suffering. Her heart suffered grievously with her Son. Even at the feet of the cross, she remained there in bitter agony, weeping, mourning and enduring piercing pains because her only Son hung upon the cross, agonising and dying on the shameful cross.

Mary remained close to Jesus to the last. Even when the other disciples had left, she remained. Mary is a model of faithfulness to the Lord. She suffered with the Lord and remained with Him until the end. No wonder she is called the Queen of Martyrs. She was co-martyred with her Son.

How faithful am I to the Lord? Am I resolved to embrace sufferings for the sake of Jesus? Am I willing to carry my own cross and follow the Lord? Am I ready to remain faithful to the Lord even at the foot of the cross? Am I resolved not to allow anything to come between me and the love of God, be it mockery, persecution, reject-tion, opposition or hatred?

Prayer
O Mary my Mother, you remained with your Son even in agony. You shared in His pains, and you didn't deny, forsake or abandon Him. Help me to remain faithful to the Lord, never to deny, forsake or abandon Him.
Amen.

Hail Holy Queen
Hail, Holy Queen, Mother of Mercy,
Hail our life, our sweetness and our hope.

To thee do we cry, O poor banished children of Eve.
To thee do we send up our sighs, mourning and
weeping in this vale of tears.
Turn then, most gracious advocate, thine eyes of
mercy towards us, and after this exile, show unto us
the blessed fruit of thy womb, Jesus.
O clement, O loving, O sweet Virgin Mary.

Intention
Let us pray for parents whose children have serious
health issues or need special care. May the agony of
Mary strengthen them, and may her prayers help
them.

Pray
One Our Father, one Hail Mary, one Glory be.

★★★★★

DAY 18

WOMAN, BEHOLD YOUR SON

25 But standing by the cross of Jesus were His mother, and His mother's sister, Mary the wife of Clopas, and Mary Magdalene. 26 When Jesus saw His mother, and the disciple whom He loved standing near, He said to His mother, "Woman, behold, your son!" 27 Then He said to the disciple, "Behold, your mother!" And from that hour the disciple took her to his own home.

JOHN 19:25-27

Reflection
As Jesus suffered on the cross, He still thought of His mother. Even on the Cross, Jesus was thinking more of the sorrows of others than of His own.

Simeon's prophecy, given at the time of Jesus' presentation at the temple had come to pass: *And a sword will pierce your own soul too* (Luke 2:35).We can only imagine the sense of grief Mary must have been feeling as she stood before Jesus and watched Him hang on the cross. Her heart must have broken at that moment.

Jesus looked out and saw His mother from the cross. He turned to John and asked him to be His substitute by caring for Mary. Yet this act of giving and receiving was not meant only for our Blessed Mother and for John, but for all of us as well. Jesus demonstrates for us the priority of family and our responsibility to them and for them – both our blood families and our family in the Church, of whom Mary is mother.

He invites us all to take Mary as our Blessed Mother and she, in turn, looks to each of us with love and affection, seeing her own precious child in each one of us.

So let us ask ourselves, do we turn to Mary, to love her and receive her motherly guidance and care? Do we allow her to embrace us and to welcome us into her heart?

If we wish to be members of God's Kingdom, we must lovingly accept Mary as our mother. All who honour Mary in this world, will be honoured by Her in the next.

Prayer
Mary, our Blessed Mother, I accept you into the home of my heart to be my spiritual mother. I accept you as my queen and seek your maternal care and guidance. Draw me closer to your divine Son and pray for me that I may seek Him above all else in life. Amen.

Hail Holy Queen
Hail, Holy Queen, Mother of Mercy,
Hail our life, our sweetness and our hope.
To thee do we cry, O poor banished children of Eve.
To thee do we send up our sighs, mourning and weeping in this vale of tears.
Turn then, most gracious advocate, thine eyes of mercy towards us,
and after this exile, show unto us the blessed fruit of thy womb, Jesus.
O clement, O loving, O sweet Virgin Mary.

Intention
Let us pray for those who have struggles within their families. May they look to Mary, our Blessed Mother and open themselves up to her love and guidance.

Pray
One Our Father, one Hail Mary, one Glory be.

DAY 19

MARY REMAINED WITH THE COMMUNITY OF BELIEVERS

12 Then they returned to Jerusalem from the mount called Olivet, which is near Jerusalem, a sabbath day's journey away. 13 When they had entered the city, they went to the room upstairs where they were staying, Peter, and John, and James, and Andrew, Philip and Thomas, Bartholomew and Matthew, James son of Alphaeus, and Simon the Zealot, and Judas son of James. 14 All these were constantly devoting themselves to prayer, together with certain women, including Mary the mother of Jesus, as well as His brothers.

ACTS 1:12-14

Reflection

Even after the death of the Lord, Mary remained with the believers. She was praying with them, and she was with them on that day when the Holy Spirit came upon them.

After the death of her Son and knowing how the disciples deserted Him, Mary could have dissociated herself from the disciples or as a bitter reaction to the agonising loss of her Son, she could have expunged herself from the community of the faithful, just as many people do today. Many are those who took offence at some things in the Church and stayed away from the assembly of the faithful.

Mary remained with the community of the faithful, praying with them, offering them counsel, support and playing her role as a mother to them all.

From Mary, let us learn to always be united with the community of faithful in prayers. Let us not allow conflict, disagreement or any form of problem, cause us to dissociate us from the Church, abandon our faith or turn our backs against the Church, which is the bride of Christ. Like Mary, let us seek to be present with the Church in her prayers and take an active part in working for her growth and the fulfilment of her mission.

Prayer

Mary my Mother, you remained with the followers of your Son even after His death. The betrayal and cowardice of the friends of your Son was not enough to make you abandon their gathering. Help me to remain committed to Christ through the Church, to pray with the community of the faithful and seek to contribute to the growth of the Church and her mission.

Amen.

Hail Holy Queen

Hail, Holy Queen, Mother of Mercy,

Hail our life, our sweetness and our hope.

To thee do we cry, O poor banished children of Eve.

To thee do we send up our sighs, mourning and weeping in this vale of tears.

Turn then, most gracious advocate, thine eyes of mercy towards us,

and after this exile, show unto us the blessed fruit of thy womb, Jesus.

O clement, O loving, O sweet Virgin Mary.

Intention

Let us pray for unity in the Church and for a revival of faith and zeal in her members.

Pray

One Our Father, one Hail Mary, one Glory be.

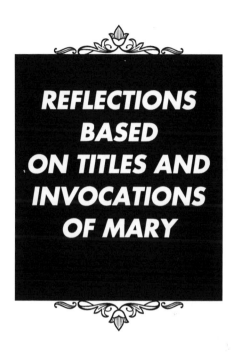

**REFLECTIONS
BASED
ON TITLES AND
INVOCATIONS
OF MARY**

DAY 20

MARY, THE NEW EVE

Adam named his wife Eve, because she would become the mother of all the living.

GENESIS 3:20

Reflection

Mary is invoked under the title of the New Eve. Just as Eve is the mother of all who lived, Mary is the Mother of the New Man through whom all are born into a new life.

Eve was a virgin and undefiled, but she conceived the word of the serpent and brought forth disobedience and death. Through Eve's disobedience to God and

Adam's cooperation with her, they lost sanctifying grace for themselves and their offspring.

Like Eve, Mary was created full of grace. But unlike Eve, Mary remained obedient to God, just as Christ, unlike Adam, remained obedient to God. In cooperation with God, Mary became Mother of the Redeemer and, in cooperation with Christ, she became Mother of the redeemed as well.

The phrase 'New Eve' or similar expressions occur in the early Church Fathers. Take, for example, Justin Martyr, who wrote within a couple of generations of the Apostles. In his *Dialogue with Trypho the Jew* (ca. A.D. 150), Justin explains that Christ destroyed Satan's work in the same way evil originally entered the world. Evil entered through Eve while she was still a virgin; so too salvation entered through Mary while she was still a virgin. Each woman willingly participated in the act they performed. Neither was an unconscious instrument. Eve listened to the serpent and conceived death. Mary listened to the Angel Gabriel and conceived life. Justin sees this clearly in Luke 1:38, when Mary says, "Let it be to me according to your Word." Thus, for Justin, Christ's becoming a man involved His Mother's willing cooperation in undoing the tangled web of sin that Eve introduced.

The key virtue here is obedience. Let us ask ourselves today, am I living a life of obedience to God or a life of rebellion? Do I live my life according to the living Word of God? Am I attentive to my conscience? Am I keen on doing what I know to be right? Do I faithfully obey the commandments of God and His Church? Do I obey the prompting of the Holy Spirit and heed His instructions? Do I reflect the obedience of Mary or the weakness of Eve?

Prayer
Holy Mother, full of grace, through your obedience, you reversed the evil that was caused by the disobedience of Eve. Help me to be obedient to God and to be docile to His Spirit that lives within me. Amen.

Hail Holy Queen
Hail, Holy Queen, Mother of Mercy,
Hail our life, our sweetness and our hope.
To thee do we cry, O poor banished children of Eve.
To thee do we send up our sighs, mourning and weeping in this vale of tears.
Turn then, most gracious advocate, thine eyes of mercy towards us,
and after this exile, show unto us the blessed fruit of thy womb, Jesus.
O clement, O loving, O sweet Virgin Mary.

Intention

Let us pray for difficult children; children who have chosen the path of arrogance and waywardness. May the prayers of Our Lady help to restore them.

Pray

One Our Father, one Hail Mary, one Glory be.

DAY 21

MARY, VIRGIN MOST PURE

3 Who shall ascend the hill of the Lord?
And who shall stand in His holy place?
4 Those who have clean hands and pure hearts,
who do not lift up their souls to what is false,
and do not swear deceitfully.
5 They will receive blessing from the Lord,
and vindication from the God of their salvation.
6 Such is the company of those who seek Him,
who seek the face of the God of Jacob.

PSALM 24:3-6

Reflection

Mary is invoked under the title 'Virgin most Pure. By her 'purity' we mean Mary's complete, self-donation, body and soul, in faith and love to God alone.

According to early Christian tradition, also contained in the second century apocryphal Gospel called *The Proto-Evangelium of James*, as a youth, Mary had resolved to follow a divine calling to consecrated virginity, as a complete self-donation to God (tradition has it that St. Joseph, too, resolved to join her in the virginal life). That is why she asked the angel to explain "how" she would bring forth a son without turning her back on her vocation.

The angel had told her that she was soon to conceive a child. According to a straightforward, literal translation of the original Greek of St. Luke's Gospel, Mary replied: "How can this be, since I do not know man?" If Mary had not already dedicated herself to a virginal life, then Gabriel might well have responded to her: "You know very well how this shall be, since you are already engaged to be married. You are soon to be united to your husband in conjugal love, and the fruit of your union will be the conception of a child."

Whether or not she vowed to be consecrated to God as a virgin, we know from her discussion with the Angel Gabriel that Mary had kept her body and mind pure and undefiled. The Angel Gabriel called her "full of grace," and one hardly can be completely "full" of divine grace if one's heart is even partially filled with disordered desires.

The virtue of purity is something God requires of all of us. Purity in our words, thoughts and actions. Purity also includes not allowing anything to take the place of God as our first and supreme love.

Like Mary, let us avoid every sin that can corrupt or defile our heart, which is the temple of the Holy Spirit. Let us firmly resist any form of impurity and consecrate our senses to God and direct them to be used for His glory alone.

Prayer
Virgin most pure, obtain for me the virtue of purity. Help me to battle against every form and appearance of impure thoughts, words, desires or actions. May my heart be a temple fit for you always.
Amen.

Hail Holy Queen
Hail, Holy Queen, Mother of Mercy,
Hail our life, our sweetness and our hope.
To thee do we cry, O poor banished children of Eve.
To thee do we send up our sighs, mourning and weeping in this vale of tears.
Turn then, most gracious advocate, thine eyes of mercy towards us, and after this exile, show unto us the blessed fruit of thy womb, Jesus.

O clement, O loving, O sweet Virgin Mary.

Intention
Let us pray for those addicted to the sin of the flesh. May the Lord deliver them and restore them to a life of grace and holiness.

Pray
One Our Father, one Hail Mary, one Glory be.

DAY 22

MARY, A FAITHFUL STEWARD

45 *"Who then is the faithful and wise slave, whom his master has put in charge of his household, to give the other slaves[a] their allowance of food at the proper time?* **46** *Blessed is that slave whom his master will find at work when he arrives.* **47** *Truly I tell you, he will put that one in charge of all his possessions.*

MATTHEW 24:45-47

Reflection

When the fullness of time came, God sent His Son to be born of Mary. Mary was chosen by the Trinity to be the Mother of the second person of the Trinity; to perform for Him the roles of a mother.

Mary became a servant of the Lord entrusted with the care of God's greatest gift to humanity. She was the mother of her Lord. Mary diligently performed her duty without failing. She was a wise and faithful steward, she did not disappoint God, she was never irresponsible or negligent. Mary is a model of faithfulness in God's service and an example of what it means to be very responsible and faithful.

Let us ask ourselves, how responsible am I with what God has entrusted to me? My family, position, assignment, resources, my gifts, my vocation, my life, even mother earth which is our common home? Let us keep in mind that we shall render an account to God concerning how we have taken care of everything He has entrusted to us.

Prayer
O Holy and Faithful Mother, you proved yourself a wise, faithful and trustworthy steward. Help me to be a trustworthy steward of all that God has vouchsafed to me.
Amen.

Hail Holy Queen
Hail, Holy Queen, Mother of Mercy,
Hail our life, our sweetness and our hope.
To thee do we cry, O poor banished children of Eve.
To thee do we send up our sighs, mourning and weeping in this vale of tears.

Turn then, most gracious advocate, thine eyes of mercy towards us,
and after this exile, show unto us the blessed fruit of thy womb, Jesus.
O clement, O loving, O sweet Virgin Mary.

Intention
Let us pray for those in authority, for religious and civil leaders, that they may be faithful and responsible stewards of their offices and opportunities.

Pray
One Our Father, one Hail Mary, one Glory be.

DAY 23

MARY, QUEEN OF SORROWS

33 And the child's father and mother were amazed at what was being said about Him. 34 Then Simeon blessed them and said to His mother Mary, "This child is destined for the falling and the rising of many in Israel, and to be a sign that will be opposed 35 so that the inner thoughts of many will be revealed—and a sword will pierce your own soul too."

LUKE 2:33-35

Reflection
In accepting to be the Mother of the Saviour of the world, Mary also accepted to carry her cross with her Son. Simeon already told her that she would suffer in her heart and soul and this she intensely did.

The sorrow of Our Lady is traditionally called the seven sorrows, but we know her suffering and sorrows cannot be numbered or measured. Let us meditate on these seven sorrows.

I.   Simeon prophesied that her Son would cause the rising and falling of many and that a sword would pierce her soul too.

II.   Mary had to flee to Egypt with Joseph and her Son in order to escape the evil scheme of Herod.

III.   For three days, she endured sleepless nights and sadness when Jesus was missing.

IV.   Mary met her Son being publicly disgraced, beaten and carrying His cross to a place of condemnation. Mary expressed her immense sorrow to St. Bridget of Sweden telling her, "By the footsteps of my Son, I knew where He had passed, for along the way the ground was marked with blood."

V.   Mary watched her Son die on the cross. She suffered the loss of her only Son. St. John Chrysostom said: "Anyone who had been present then on Mount Calvary, would have seen two altars on which two great sacrifices were being offered - the one in the body of Jesus and the other in the heart of Mary."

VI. Mary held the lifeless body of her Son being taken down from the cross.

VII. She watched her Son being buried in the tomb.

Dear friends, let us always reflect on the sorrows of Our Lady and let these move us to gratitude and compassion. Let us be encouraged in our own moments of sorrow, that our suffering doesn't mean that we are not loved by God and let us confidently have recourse to Our Lady who is acquainted with suffering and grief to help us in our sorrows and dark moments.

Prayer
O most sorrowful Mother, I meditate on your suffering today and I am moved to compassion. Thank you for all you endured out of love. Obtain for me the grace of endurance and final perseverance so that whatever may befall me in life, I may never separate myself from your Son.
Amen.

Hail Holy Queen
Hail, Holy Queen, Mother of Mercy,
Hail our life, our sweetness and our hope.
To thee do we cry, O poor banished children of Eve.
To thee do we send up our sighs, mourning and weeping in this vale of tears.
Turn then, most gracious advocate, thine eyes of mercy towards us,

and after this exile, show unto us the blessed fruit of thy womb, Jesus.

O clement, O loving, O sweet Virgin Mary.

Intention

Let us pray for those who are unwell, those in so much pain. May the sorrows of Our Lady comfort them.

Pray

One Our Father, one Hail Mary, one Glory be.

★★★★★

DAY 24

MARY AS A REFUGE OF SINNERS

7 After the Lord had said these things to Job, He said to Eliphaz the Temanite, "I am angry with you and your two friends, because you have not said what is right about me, as my servant Job did. 8 Now take seven bulls and seven male sheep, and go to my servant Job, and offer a burnt offering for yourselves. My servant Job will pray for you, and I will listen to his prayer. Then I will not punish you for being foolish. You have not said what is right about me, as my servant Job did." 9 So Eliphaz the Temanite, Bildad the Shuhite, and Zophar the Naamathite did as the Lord said, and the Lord listened to Job's prayer.

JOB 42:7-9

Reflection

In the Litany of Loreto, Mary is invoked under the title 'Refuge of Sinners.' Its use goes back to Saint Germanus of Constantinople in the 8th century. Our hope of mercy is in Jesus and His atoning sacrifice for us. However, the Lord has also made Mary a veritable help for sinners. She is a compassionate, holy and chaste Mother of the Saviour. She is able to and indeed she has continued to be a refuge to poor sinners who have recourse to her.

Just as Job prayed for his friends and God forgave them, the Lord has also given our Blessed Mother to us as our intercessor. Mary obtains for sinners, true and sincere conversion. She obtains mercy from God for us and the grace we need to rise from the mire of sin. Anyone who has recourse to her is never left unaided. It is, therefore, a salutary practice for us to run to her for the conversion of sinners, to ask her to obtain clemency from God, to disarm the just anger of God caused by our sins and also to obtain the grace to overcome the power of sin.

Today, let us ask ourselves, God has given us a refuge in Mary, her maternal mantle can preserve us from the wrath of divine justice, but then do we genuinely hate sin? Are we passionate about the conversion of sinners? Do we recognise the malice of sin and our need for God's grace? Do we confidently approach Our Lady for help?

Prayer

Dearest Mother of my Saviour, I confess you as a sure refuge of sinners. I come to you as a sinner. Obtain for me, hatred for sin, mercy from your Son and the grace to overcome every temptation of sin.
Amen.

Hail Holy Queen

Hail, Holy Queen, Mother of Mercy,
Hail our life, our sweetness and our hope.
To thee do we cry, O poor banished children of Eve.
To thee do we send up our sighs, mourning and weeping in this vale of tears.
Turn then, most gracious advocate, thine eyes of mercy towards us,
and after this exile, show unto us the blessed fruit of thy womb, Jesus.
O clement, O loving, O sweet Virgin Mary.

Intention

Let us pray for the conversion of hardened sinners and enemies of the Church.

Pray

One Our Father, one Hail Mary, one Glory be.

★★★★★

DAY 25

MARY AS A VESSEL OF HONOUR

20 In a great house there are not only vessels of gold and silver but also of wood and earthenware, and some for noble use, some for ignoble. 21 If anyone purifies himself from what is ignoble, then he will be a vessel for noble use, consecrated and useful to the master of the house, ready for good work. 22 So shun youthful passions and aim at righteousness, faith, love, and peace, along with those who call upon the Lord from a pure heart.

2 TIMOTHY 2:20-22

Reflection

The Blessed Virgin Mary is venerated with the title 'Vessel of Honour.' She was sinless, pure of heart and she belonged wholly and entirely to the Lord, submitting to His will. She was chosen by God and filled not only with God's heavenly and holy grace, but also with the Son of God. Like her, each one of us should also be a vessel of honour, for we receive Our Lord in Holy Communion. After Holy Communion we are all saturated with Jesus.

In the New Testament, Christians are described as chosen vessels, each created by God. He chose us and He has a plan for each of us, just as He had for Mary. We are vessels to be saturated with God's love and His Word. We are vessels to be poured out every day for His purpose if we, like Mary, submit ourselves to His will.

Let us then consider this; as vessels of honour are we honourable in all our dealings, true, straight and just? Do we behave in a way that is ignoble and degrading to ourselves? Do we allow ourselves to become saturated with Jesus and ready for good work or do we allow ourselves to become empty?

Let us pray that we also may deserve to be called, each in our own degree, "vessels of honour."

Prayer

Holy Mary, Vessel of Honour, we venerate you for carrying our Lord Jesus Christ into the world. Look with favour on us as we struggle to become 'vessels of honour' and guide us towards submitting to God's will for our lives, rather than our own.
Amen.

Hail Holy Queen

Hail, Holy Queen, Mother of Mercy,
Hail our life, our sweetness and our hope.
To thee do we cry, O poor banished children of Eve.
To thee do we send up our sighs, mourning and weeping in this vale of tears.
Turn then, most gracious advocate, thine eyes of mercy towards us,
and after this exile, show unto us the blessed fruit of thy womb, Jesus.
O clement, O loving, O sweet Virgin Mary

Intention

Let us pray for those struggling to open their hearts to God in gratitude, praise and worship and ask Him to fill them with His Holy Spirit.

Pray

One Our Father, one Hail Mary, one Glory be.

★★★★★

DAY 26

MARY, MODEL OF GENTLENESS

Blessed are the meek for they shall inherit the earth
MATTHEW 5:5

Reflection

Mary is a role model, for all Christians, of gentle yet courageous faith, dedication and love. She was chosen by God and she willingly submitted to His will and became the mother of Jesus as well as our Heavenly Mother. In her life, she was gentle and mild, considerate and thoughtful of others (think about her visit to her cousin Elizabeth and the Wedding at Cana). She never spoke a word of anger, not even to those who executed her Son. She embraced all situations with calmness and serenity.

On submitting to God's will, Mary was filled with the Holy Spirit. Gentleness is a fruit of the Holy Spirit and is a powerful way of witnessing to our faith and our convictions.

In the fast-paced world of today, we may forget to be gentle. We may even forget how important it is to be gentle. A gentle person is not weak; they have their power and strength under control and treat everyone with kindness and understanding. Wisdom comes through a gentle spirit and a peaceful mind.

Let us ask ourselves, how considerate am I of the feelings of others in my dealings with them? Do I think about what I say before I say it, or does what is in my mind come out unedited? Do I think before I act? Do I behave reasonably, or do I react hastily, rashly or violently?

As we contemplate the fruit of gentleness, let us keep the example and model of Mary, our gentle heavenly mother in our hearts.

Prayer

O gentle Mother of Christ, you are a role model for us of gentleness, faithfulness and trust. Help me to treat all people and things with loving gentleness. May I learn to be patient, loving and kind always,

slow to anger and rich in compassion. Help me to seek a quiet calm so that I may hear God's truth in my heart.
Amen.

Hail Holy Queen
Hail, Holy Queen, Mother of Mercy,
Hail our life, our sweetness and our hope.
To thee do we cry, O poor banished children of Eve.
To thee do we send up our sighs, mourning and weeping in this vale of tears.
Turn then, most gracious advocate, thine eyes of mercy towards us,
and after this exile, show unto us the blessed fruit of thy womb, Jesus.
O clement, O loving, O sweet Virgin Mary.

Intention
Let us pray for the women, men and children who daily suffer the effects of war, violence and the lack of gentleness in our world and in their lives.

Pray
One Our Father, one Hail Mary, one Glory be.

★★★★★

DAY 27

MARY, QUEEN OF FAMILIES

51 Then He went down with them and came to Nazareth and was obedient to them. His mother treasured all these things in her heart.

LUKE 2:51

Reflection.

Our Lady is the Queen of all families. She is invoked under this title whenever we say the litany. This invocation flows naturally from the fact that Mary is Mother of the Church. The family is considered the 'domestic Church', since it is there that the seed of faith which is planted in the Sacrament of Baptism is nourished and flourished by the teaching and good example of the parents and members of the home.

The family is the smallest cell of the Church which builds up the Mystical Body of Christ. It is in the family that we find the first school of prayer and the moral and social virtues that form the basis for society. The family is the place which builds up the world by guarding and transmitting virtues and values from parent to child by what is taught and lived.

Mary played an important role in the Holy family, which is the model of all families. She played a significant role in raising her Son, our Saviour, Jesus Christ. By giving Mary to John on the cross, Mary is given to every Christian family to take her in and allow her to help them as they journey through the difficult task of making their families a domestic Church and a place where life is respected, faith is nurtured, and love is shared; a place where everyone has a safe environment to flourish.

We are therefore invited to consciously create a space for Mary as the queen of our homes. Let us as a family have recourse to her intercession, sing in honour of her, have an altar in her honour, adorn our house with her pictures and statues, honour her by praying the rosary and ponder always on her heroic sacrifice for humanity and her excellent virtues.

Prayer

Mary, Queen of all families, I honour, love and enthrone you as the Queen of my heart and my home. May the peace and love that flow in the Holy family flow also in my home and in my life.
Amen.

Hail Holy Queen

Hail, Holy Queen, Mother of Mercy,

Hail our life, our sweetness and our hope.

To thee do we cry, O poor banished children of Eve.

To thee do we send up our sighs, mourning and weeping in this vale of tears.

Turn then, most gracious advocate, thine eyes of mercy towards us,

and after this exile, show unto us the blessed fruit of thy womb, Jesus.

O clement, O loving, O sweet Virgin Mary.

Intention

Let us pray for peace, love and joy in every family and for Our Lady's intercession in every home divided by conflict, hatred and bitterness.

Pray

One Our Father, one Hail Mary, one Glory be.

★★★★★

DAY 28

MARY, TERROR OF DEMONS

3 Then another portent appeared in heaven: a great red dragon, with seven heads and ten horns, and seven diadems on his heads. 4 His tail swept down a third of the stars of heaven and threw them to the earth. Then the dragon stood before the woman who was about to bear a child, so that he might devour her child as soon as it was born. 5 And she gave birth to a son, a male child, who is to rule all the nations with a rod of iron. But her child was snatched away and taken to God and to his throne.

REVELATION 12:3-5

Reflection

Mary is the New Eve that reversed the damage caused by the first Eve. Mary is the channel through whom the Saviour of mankind came to the world, the Saviour who would destroy the work of the devil.

Mary is a refuge of sinners and a powerful intercessor. Through her many people have been rescued from damnation and she has obtained graces for many people to overcome the temptation, wiles and snares of the enemy.

Mary plays a role that upsets the devil and opposes his schemes and agenda. He is willing to do everything to oppose devotion to her, to discourage people from having recourse to her. The devil is ready to do everything to attack her and to raise up people who would speak against her and cause hatred and confusion in the hearts of so many.

Sadly, many in our age today are now speaking against love for and devotion to the Blessed Mother of Jesus. Many are planting the seed of hatred in the heart of others against her. These are clear evidence of the work of the enemy who will stop at nothing to stop people from running to this channel of grace.

Dear friends, let us with equal and unrivalled passion proclaim the power of Our Lady's intercession. It is not enough to have recourse to her, let us talk about it, praise her to others and help people to discover the graces we can obtain through her. Let us oppose the work and agenda of the evil one.

Prayer

O Blessed Virgin Mary, you are a terror to the devil and a major obstacle in his plan for the eternal damnation of all souls. Continue dear Mother, to put the devil to shame, save more souls from the fires of hell, and lead more souls to heaven, especially those in most need of your mercy.
Amen.

Hail Holy Queen

Hail, Holy Queen, Mother of Mercy,
Hail our life, our sweetness and our hope.
To thee do we cry, O poor banished children of Eve.
To thee do we send up our sighs, mourning and weeping in this vale of tears.
Turn then, most gracious advocate, thine eyes of mercy towards us, and after this exile, show unto us the blessed fruit of thy womb, Jesus.
O clement, O loving, O sweet Virgin Mary.

Intention

Let us pray that the Lord will deliver all who have sold their souls to the devil by their membership in satanic societies and groups who are opposed to the Christian faith.

Pray

One Our Father, one Hail Mary, one Glory be.

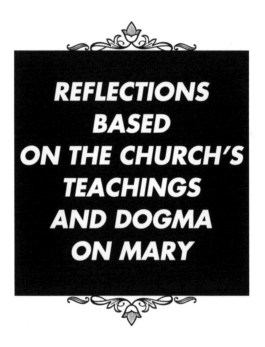

**REFLECTIONS
BASED
ON THE CHURCH'S
TEACHINGS
AND DOGMA
ON MARY**

DAY 29

THE IMMACULATE CONCEPTION

For He chose us in Him before the creation of the world to be holy and blameless in His sight.

EPHESIANS 1:4

Reflection

Mary was conceived immaculately without any stain or guilt of sin. This was God's way of preparing her to be the vessel through whom the one who was to save us from sin would be born. The one who is to restore our human nature to its original innocence, shared in a human nature that was perfect, innocent, undefiled and unstained by sin.

This doctrine was universally believed over the centuries but was proclaimed a dogma in 1854 by Pope Pius IX. To confirm this doctrine, four years after the proclamation, precisely on March 25, 1858, Our Lady appeared to St. Bernadette at Lourdes and pronounced her name as the Immaculate Conception.

To preserve Mary from the stain of sin is to testify to the fact that sin is the greatest evil. The vessel through whom Christ must be born must therefore be undefiled by it.

Even though we are conceived in sin, the Lord wants to give us grace to battle with sin. Just as Mary was purified for the sake of her mission and the mission of her Son, the Lord wants each of us also to distance ourselves from sin and its corruption. He wants us to constantly purify ourselves so that we can approach His presence with a clear conscience and make ourselves worthy for His purpose.

Do I make the effort to battle against sin? Do I search my conscience and make good and regular confession with firm resolution to avoid what offends the holiness of God? Am I careful enough to avoid not just sins but occasions that could lead me to sin? Do I dread offending the holiness and love of God? Do I watch over my life most carefully so that sin does not obscure the glory of God present in my earthenware vessel?

Prayer

O most chaste and pure virgin, help me to avoid anything that can defile the temple of the Spirit that is within me. May I seek to be holy and blameless before my Creator.

Amen.

Hail Holy Queen

Hail, Holy Queen, Mother of Mercy,
Hail our life, our sweetness and our hope.
To thee do we cry, O poor banished children of Eve.
To thee do we send up our sighs, mourning and weeping in this vale of tears.
Turn then, most gracious advocate, thine eyes of mercy towards us,
and after this exile, show unto us the blessed fruit of thy womb, Jesus.
O clement, O loving, O sweet Virgin Mary.

Intention

Let us pray for hardened sinners that through the intercession of our Lady immaculately conceived, the Lord may restore them to a life of righteousness and holiness.

Pray

One Our Father, one Hail Mary, one Glory be.

★★★★★

DAY 30

THE GLORIOUS ASSUMPTION

9 Therefore my heart is glad and my tongue rejoices; my body also will rest secure, 10 because you will not abandon me to the grave, nor will you let your Holy One see decay. 11 You have made known to me the path of life; you will fill me with joy in your presence, with eternal pleasures at your right hand.

PSALM 16:9-11

Reflection
Today, let us reflect on the Assumption of the Blessed Virgin Mary. After the completion of her earthly life, Mary was taken up to heaven, body and

soul. She was preserved from decay because her body was without the least stain of sin.

The doctrine of the assumption has always been taught and believed by the early Church, however, it was promulgated as a dogma of faith by Pope Pius XII on November 1, 1950 in his apostolic constitution entitled *Munifentissimus Deus*. Her assumption is a reward for the total surrender of her will and her cooperation with God to play her part in the eternal plan for the redemption of humankind.

The assumption of our Mother Mary is a reminder to us all that all who serve the Lord diligently shall be rewarded. We shall share in the glory and power of the resurrection. The Lord will raise us to Himself and call us to share in His glory.

Let us seek then to serve God diligently on earth and to glorify Him, so that at death our souls shall also be raised to share in the eternal happiness of heaven.

Prayer

O Queen and Mother, you were assumed into heaven as a reward for your faithfulness and complete submission to the Father. Grant we pray, that we may also be obedient and faithful, and may our death also be a glorious passage from life to eternal life.
Amen.

Hail Holy Queen

Hail, Holy Queen, Mother of Mercy,

Hail our life, our sweetness and our hope.

To thee do we cry, O poor banished children of Eve.

To thee do we send up our sighs, mourning and weeping in this vale of tears.

Turn then, most gracious advocate, thine eyes of mercy towards us,

and after this exile, show unto us the blessed fruit of thy womb, Jesus.

O clement, O loving, O sweet Virgin Mary.

Intention

Let us pray for the dying, that they may see Christ before they see death.

Pray

One Our Father, one Hail Mary, one Glory be.

★★★★★

DAY 31

THE CROWNING OF OUR LADY

A great portent appeared in heaven: a woman clothed with the sun, with the moon under her feet, and on her head a crown of twelve stars.

REVELATION 12:1

Reflection
Mary is the Mother of the King of kings, the Lamb upon the throne. While on earth she nurtured our Lord Jesus Christ and was His holy and devout mother. Now she shares in the glory of her Son who is King in heaven and on earth.

After the completion of her earthly journey and mission, she was received into the glory of paradise and received the crown of unfading glory which the Lord, the righteous judge, has kept for all who shall remain faithful to the end.

As we reflect on the glory of our Blessed Mother in heaven and her glorious coronation, let us be encouraged in our own life's struggles that when the battle of life is over, we shall wear the crown of glory in the new Jerusalem.

Prayer
Our Mother, Queen of all Saints, you have been crowned with glory and honour in heaven. We beg you to ensure that we do not derail from the right path and we do not miss the crown of glory awaiting each of us in heaven.
Amen.

Hail Holy Queen
Hail, Holy Queen, Mother of Mercy,
Hail our life, our sweetness and our hope.
To thee do we cry, O poor banished children of Eve.
To thee do we send up our sighs, mourning and weeping in this vale of tears.
Turn then, most gracious advocate, thine eyes of mercy towards us, and after this exile, show unto us the blessed fruit of thy womb, Jesus.
O clement, O loving, O sweet Virgin Mary.

Intention
Let us pray for souls in purgatory. May our prayers bring them relief and release.

Pray
One Our Father, one Hail Mary, one Glory be.

*****

PRAYERS IN HONOUR OF OUR LADY

THE HOLY ROSARY WITH MEDITATIONS AND DIFFERENT INTENTIONS

Make the sign of the cross
In the name of the Father, and of the Son, and of the Holy Spirit.
Amen.

The Apostles' Creed
I believe in God, the Father almighty, Creator of heaven and earth, and in Jesus Christ, His only Son, our Lord, who was conceived by the Holy Spirit, born of the Virgin Mary, suffered under Pontius Pilate, was crucified, died and was buried; He descended into hell; on the third day He rose again from the dead; He ascended into heaven, and is seated at the right hand of God the Father almighty; from there He will come to judge the living and the dead. I believe in the Holy Spirit, the holy Catholic Church, the communion of saints, the forgiveness of sins, the resurrection of the body, and life everlasting.
Amen.

Our Father

Our Father, who art in heaven, hallowed be Thy name; Thy kingdom come; Thy will be done on earth as it is in heaven. Give us this day our daily bread; and forgive us our trespasses as we forgive those who trespass against us; and lead us not into temptation but deliver us from evil.

Amen.

Three Hail Marys

Hail Mary, full of grace. The Lord is with thee. Blessed art thou amongst women, and blessed is the fruit of thy womb, Jesus. Holy Mary, Mother of God, pray for us sinners, now and at the hour of our death.

Amen.

Glory be

Glory be to the Father and to the Son, and to the Holy Spirit, as it was in the beginning, is now, and ever shall be, world without end.

Amen.

The Fatima Prayer

O my Jesus, forgive us our sins, save us from the fires of hell, and lead all souls to heaven, especially those in most need of Your Mercy.

Amen.

THE JOYFUL MYSTERIES WITH MEDITATIONS AND PRAYERS
(Monday and Saturday)

I. The Annunciation
The Angel Gabriel was sent to announce to Mary that God had chosen her to be the mother of the expected Messiah. Mary agreed to surrender her will, her womb, her life, totally to God. Through you O Mother of the Word incarnate, I have learnt that I belong totally to God, and to live must be to live for Him.

Lord, teach me to be willing like our Blessed Mother to surrender all I have and all I am to you always.
Amen.

II. Mary Visited Her Cousin Elizabeth
Mary hastened to the hill country of Judea to visit her cousin Elizabeth. The presence of Mary in this home brought great joy, not just to Elizabeth but also the child in her womb. O what joy Mary brings to every home and heart where she is welcomed.

Lord Jesus, help me to grow in love for your Mother, may I never be deprived of her maternal charity and succour.
Amen.

III. The Birth of Our Lord Jesus
Jesus is the Only Begotten Son of God, God from God, one in substance with the Father. He was born

as a helpless baby in a manger in Bethlehem. God the Son came as a baby. What incomprehensible mystery of divine love and humility. Who can fathom this mystery?

Lord, let me keep the mystery of your incarnation always before me, that I may learn and practice true humility, sacrifice and love.
Amen.

IV. The Presentation of the Child Jesus in the Temple

According to the Jewish custom, Jesus was presented in the temple. Simeon was filled with great joy upon seeing the Lord and holding the child in his arms, he said, "Now O Lord, you can dismiss your servant in peace, for my eyes have seen your salvation..."

What great joy it must have been for Simeon to hold in his arms the one who holds the whole world in His arms, but the greatest joy is to receive our Lord and our God into our very heart.

Lord Jesus, open my eyes to see the divine hidden in the mundane. Open the eyes of my mind to see your profound majesty and glory often veiled in simplicity.
Amen.

V. The Finding of the Child Jesus in the Temple

After three days of painful searching, the parents of Jesus found Him in the temple, sitting among the teachers, listening to them and asking them questions. Imagine the sorrow of the parents of Jesus while they searched for Him for three days. Consider their joy upon finding Him. How beautiful to behold the Godchild in the temple; the true temple of God sitting inside the temple made by human hands.

Lord Jesus, do not ever permit me to be separated from you in time or in eternity. Without you my life will be unbearably empty and hopeless.
Amen.

THE SORROWFUL MYSTERIES WITH MEDITATIONS AND PRAYERS
(Tuesday and Friday)

I. The Prayer and Agony in the Garden of Gethsemane

In the Garden of Gethsemane, Jesus knelt down and prayed with bitter anguish. His sweat became like drops of blood falling down on the ground. He said "Father, if you are willing, remove this cup from me; yet, not my will but yours be done."

What great pain Jesus must have felt, foreseeing the heavy burden of sin and punishment of mankind about to be placed on His shoulders, and yet He was ready to accept it all as His Father's will.

Lord Jesus, teach me also to submit to the Father's will for me in all things, for in His will is my peace. **Amen.**

II. The Scourging at the Pillar

Jesus was fiercely scourged by the drunken soldiers. They took turns to flog Him merci-lessly, until His back was covered with blood, bruises and open wounds. He was as one from whom people hide their faces. Yet, He was wounded for our transgressions, crushed for our iniquities.

Lord Jesus, for me you were scourged, your body was totally disfigured, you paid the price for my sins.

Instil in me hatred for sin and love for the one who suffered so much for me.
Amen.

III. The Crowning with Thorns

Jesus was stripped of His garment and a scarlet robe was put on Him. The soldiers then twisted some sharp thorns into a crown, and they forced it on His head. They put a reed in His right hand and knelt before Him and mocked Him, saying 'Hail, King of the Jews!' The King of kings and Lord of lords was crowned with thorns, His holy and sacred head thus brutally injured.

Lord Jesus, you were crowned with thorns so that I may receive the crown of unfading glory. May I spend every moment of my life thanking You for all you've done for me.
Amen.

IV. Jesus Carries His Cross

Jesus accepted the heavy cross; He placed on His shoulder the weight of the sins of the whole of humanity. Three times He fell because of the crushing weight of the cross and the brutal treatment of the soldiers, but then He staggered on to Calvary.

Lord Jesus, help me to embrace my cross of life with a new understanding, faith, courage and resignation to your will. May I follow in faithfulness to the one who carried the cross of my sin.

Amen.

V. The Crucifixion and Death of Jesus

When they got to Golgotha, the soldiers crucified Jesus. Over His head they put the inscription, 'this is Jesus, the King of the Jews.' Those who passed by derided Him; His enemies mocked Him. At the foot of His cross were His mother and His beloved disciple, suffering with Him. At three o'clock in the afternoon, the Lord of life tasted death so that we who are dead in sin, may come to life.

Lord Jesus, for my sake, You died on the cross. Help me to die to sin and rise with you to a life of righteousness.

Amen.

THE GLORIOUS MYSTERIES WITH MEDITATIONS AND PRAYERS
(Wednesday and Sunday)

I. The Resurrection of Jesus
After the crucifixion and death of Jesus, His enemies went away joyfully. His disciples went sorrowfully away too, and soldiers were stationed to guard His tomb. While in the tomb, He went into Hades to liberate the souls of the righteous who were yet unable to gain access to heaven. On the third day after destroying death and releasing his captives, Jesus rose triumphantly from the grave.

Lord Jesus by dying you destroyed death, by rising you restored life. May I experience in my life, the power and the glory of your resurrection.
Amen.

II. The Ascension of the Lord
After forty days of appearing to His disciples and preparing them for the coming Paraclete, Jesus then ascended bodily and gloriously into heaven, while the disciples watched in amazement.

Lord Jesus, you ascended into heaven not to abandon me on earth but to prepare a place for me in heaven. After my earthly sojourn is ended, may I be worthy to reign eternally with you in the kingdom of the Father.
Amen.

III. The Descent of the Holy Spirit

Ten days after the ascension of Jesus, on the Jewish feast of the Pentecost, while the apostles were praying in the upper room, Jesus sent to them the first fruit of His ascension, the promised Paraclete. The Holy Spirit was to empower, comfort, teach, direct and lead them.

Lord Jesus, just as the disciples received the Holy Spirit at Pentecost, may I enjoy always the comforting presence of the Paraclete. Do not take your Holy Spirit from me; let Him lead, inspire, direct and empower me always.
Amen.

IV. The Assumption of the Blessed Virgin Mary

After the earthly sojourn of our Blessed Mother was over, she was taken up to heaven body and soul, so that she who is the mother of the Holy Son of God, she who was conceived and who conceived Him without the least stain of sin, should be excluded from the corruption of her flesh, the sentence of decay. For in this way, she was rewarded for her cooperation with God in the redemption of humankind.

Lord Jesus, the assumption of your mother assures me that you greatly bless those who dedicate their lives to serve you faithfully. May my life on earth give

you glory, so that I will one day hear these words "come, good and faithful servant."
Amen.

V. The Coronation of Our Blessed Mother

She who is the faithful mother of Jesus, the universal King, was crowned in heaven as the queen of heaven and of earth. While in heaven, she does not forget us her children. She enjoys a special privilege by virtue of her relationship with her Son and so she can obtain for us graces necessary for our wellbeing and salvation.

Lord Jesus, you crowned your mother as queen of angels and saints and indeed all your children. Grant that I may love her with all my heart, honour her as my queen and mother, and be eternally close to her.
Amen.

THE MYSTERIES OF LIGHT WITH MEDITATIONS AND PRAYERS
(Thursday)

I. The Baptism of the Lord
Before the commencement of His public ministry, Jesus presented Himself at the River Jordan to be baptised by John. When Jesus had been baptised, just as He came up from the water, suddenly the heavens were opened and the Spirit of the Lord descended upon Him like a dove and a voice from heaven said, "this is my Son, my beloved, with whom I am well pleased."

Lord Jesus, you accepted baptism from John even though you are without sin; you associated with us in our sinful condition. May I never feel ashamed to associate with you.
Amen.

II. The Self-Revelation at the Marriage Feast at Cana in Galilee
Jesus, His mother and His disciples attended a wedding feast at Cana in Galilee. There the host ran short of wine and the mother of Jesus implored her Son to help the family. Even though His hour had not yet come, He came to their aid and turned water into sweeter and better wine, thus saving the couple from unforgettable shame.

Lord Jesus, your presence at that wedding saved the couple from shame and public reproach. May you be present in my life, in my word, thought and deed to save me from regrettable error and eternal shame. **Amen.**

III. The Proclamation of the Kingdom of God with the Call to Conversion

After the baptism of Jesus and His victory over the tempter in the wilderness, He called His disciples and He began His public ministry, teaching with authority, healing with great power, restoring light, hope, joy and life to people and doing good to all, thus proclaiming the presence of God's kingdom among us.

Lord Jesus, you went about doing good, help me to extend your goodness to those around me. May I share in your ministry not just by words, but by the example of a good life.
Amen.

IV. The Transfiguration of the Lord

Jesus took Peter, James and John to a high mountain to pray. In their presence He was transfigured; His face shone like the sun, and His clothes became dazzling white. Suddenly, Moses and Elijah appeared talking with Him.

Lord Jesus, in the presence of your disciples you were transfigured. They had a foretaste of the glory awaiting all of us when the battle of life is over. Help me to always keep in mind the glory of heaven, so

that I may, in hope, endure the cross on the way to this glory.
Amen.

V. The Institution of the Holy Eucharist

On the evening of the first day of unleavened bread when the Passover Lamb is slain, Jesus sat with His disciples to eat the Passover meal. While they were eating, He took a loaf of bread, and after the blessing, He broke it and gave it to His disciples and said, "this is my Body". Then He took a cup and after giving thanks He gave it to them saying, "this is my Blood of the covenant which is poured out for many."

Thus, He instituted the Eucharist as a sacramental expression of His Paschal mystery and as a re-enactment of His sacrifice on Calvary.

Lord Jesus, you gave your Body and Blood to your Church through your Apostles. May I always hunger to receive you in purity of heart, with faith, devotion, reverence and gratitude.
Amen.

Hail Holy Queen

Hail, Holy Queen, Mother of mercy, hail our life, our sweetness and our hope. To thee do we cry, O poor banished children of Eve. To thee do we send up our sighs, mourning and weeping in this vale of tears. Turn then, most gracious advocate, thine eyes of mercy toward us; and after this our exile show unto us the blessed fruit of thy womb Jesus. O clement, O loving, O sweet Virgin Mary.

V. Pray for us, O holy Mother of God.
R. *That we may be made worthy of the promises of Christ.*

Let us pray
O God, whose only-begotten Son, by His life, death, and resurrection, has purchased for us the rewards of eternal life; grant we beseech Thee, that by meditating upon these mysteries of the most holy Rosary of the Blessed Virgin Mary, we may imitate what they contain and obtain what they promise. Through the same Christ our Lord.
Amen.

Make the sign of the cross
In the name of the Father, and of the Son, and of the Holy Spirit.
Amen.

LITANY OF THE BLESSED VIRGIN MARY

Lord have mercy. *Lord have mercy.*
Christ have mercy. *Christ have mercy.*
Lord have mercy. *Lord have mercy.*
Christ hear us. *Christ graciously hear us.*

God, the Father of Heaven, *have mercy on us.*
God the Son, Redeemer of the world, *have mercy on us.*
God the Holy Spirit, *have mercy on us.*
Holy Trinity, One God, *have mercy on us.*

Holy Mary, *pray for us.*
Holy Mother of God, *pray for us.*
Holy Virgin of Virgins, *pray for us.*

Mother of Christ, *pray for us.*
Mother of the Church, *pray for us.*
Mother of Mercy, *pray for us.*
Mother of Divine Grace, *pray for us.*
Mother of Hope, *pray for us.*
Mother Most Pure, *pray for us.*
Mother Most Chaste, *pray for us.*
Mother Inviolate, *pray for us.*
Mother Undefiled, *pray for us.*
Mother Most Amiable, *pray for us.*
Mother Most Admirable, *pray for us.*
Mother of Good Counsel, *pray for us.*
Mother of our Creator, *pray for us.*
Mother of our Saviour, *pray for us.*

Virgin Most Prudent, *pray for us.*
Virgin Most Venerable, *pray for us.*
Virgin Most Renowned, *pray for us.*
Virgin Most Powerful, *pray for us.*
Virgin Most Merciful, *pray for us.*
Virgin Most Faithful, *pray for us.*

Mirror of Justice, *pray for us.*
Seat of Wisdom, *pray for us.*
Cause of Our Joy, *pray for us.*
Spiritual Vessel, *pray for us.*
Vessel of Honour, *pray for us.*
Singular Vessel of Devotion, *pray for us.*
Mystical Rose, *pray for us.*
Tower of David, *pray for us.*
Tower of Ivory, *pray for us.*
House of Gold, *pray for us.*
Ark of the Covenant, *pray for us.*
Gate of Heaven, *pray for us.*
Morning Star, *pray for us.*
Health of the Sick, *pray for us.*
Refuge of Sinners, *pray for us.*
Solace of Migrants, *pray for us.*
Comforter of the Afflicted, *pray for us.*
Help of Christians, *pray for us.*

Queen of Angels, *pray for us.*
Queen of Patriarchs, *pray for us.*
Queen of Prophets, *pray for us.*
Queen of Apostles, *pray for us.*
Queen of Martyrs, *pray for us.*

Queen of Confessors, *pray for us.*
Queen of Virgins, *pray for us.*
Queen of all Saints, *pray for us.*
Queen Conceived without Original Sin, *pray for us.*
Queen Assumed into Heaven, *pray for us.*
Queen of the Most Holy Rosary, *pray for us.*
Queen of Families, *pray for us.*
Queen of Peace, *pray for us.*

Lamb of God, who takes away the sins of the world, *spare us, O Lord!*
Lamb of God, who takes away the sins of the world, *graciously hear us, O Lord!*
Lamb of God, who takes away the sins of the world, *have mercy on us.*

V. Pray for us, O holy Mother of God.
R. *That we may be made worthy of the promises of Christ.*

Let us pray.
Grant, we beseech you, O Lord God, that we your servants, may enjoy lasting health of mind and body, and by the glorious intercession of the Blessed Mary, ever Virgin, be delivered from present sorrow and enter into the joy of eternal happiness. Through Christ our Lord.
Amen.

★★★★★

THE SEVEN SORROWS OF THE BLESSED VIRGIN MARY

V. O God, come to my assistance
R. *O Lord, make haste to help me*
V. Glory be to the Father, and to the Son, and to the Holy Spirit.
R. *As it was in the beginning, is now, and ever shall be, world without end.*
Amen

I. The First Sorrow: The Prophecy of Simeon
And Simeon blessed them and said to Mary His mother: Behold this child is set for the fall and for the resurrection of many in Israel, and for a sign which shall be contradicted; And thy own soul a sword shall pierce, that out of many hearts thoughts may be revealed.

LUKE 2:34-35

I grieve for thee, O Mary most sorrowful, in the affliction of thy tender heart at the prophecy of the holy and aged Simeon. Dear Mother, by thy heart so afflicted, obtain for me the virtue of humility and the gift of the holy fear of God

Pray
One Our Father and seven Hail Marys

II. The Second Sorrow: The Flight Into Egypt
And after they (the wise men) were departed, behold an angel of the Lord appeared in sleep to Joseph, saying: Arise and take the child and His mother and fly into Egypt: and be

there until I shall tell thee. For it will come to pass that Herod will seek the child to destroy Him. Who arose and took the child and His mother by night and retired into Egypt: and He was there until the death of Herod.

MATTHEW 2:13-14

I grieve for thee, O Mary most sorrowful, in the anguish of thy most affectionate heart during the flight into Egypt and thy sojourn there. Dear Mother, by thy heart so troubled, obtain for me the virtue of generosity, especially toward the poor, and the gift of piety.

Pray
One Our Father and seven Hail Marys

III. The Third Sorrow: The Loss of the Child Jesus in the Temple

And having fulfilled the days, when they returned, the Child Jesus remained in Jerusalem; and His parents knew it not. And thinking that He was in the company, they came a day's journey, and sought Him among their kinsfolk and acquaintance. And not finding Him, they returned into Jerusalem, seeking Him.

LUKE 2:43-45

I grieve for thee, O Mary most sorrowful, in those anxieties which tried thy troubled heart at the loss of thy dear Jesus. Dear Mother, by thy heart so full of anguish, obtain for me the virtue of chastity and the gift of knowledge.

122

Pray

One Our Father and seven Hail Marys

IV. The Fourth Sorrow: Mary Meets Jesus on the Way to Calvary

And there followed Him a great multitude of people, and of women, who bewailed and lamented Him.

LUKE 23:27

I grieve for thee, O Mary most sorrowful in the consternation of thy heart at meeting Jesus as He carried His Cross. Dear Mother, by thy heart so troubled, obtain for me the virtue of patience and the gift of fortitude.

Pray

One Our Father and seven Hail Marys

V. The Fifth Sorrow: Jesus Dies on the Cross

They crucified Him. Now there stood by the cross of Jesus, His Mother. When Jesus therefore had seen His Mother and the disciple standing whom He loved, He saith to His Mother: Woman: behold thy son. After that He saith to the disciple: Behold thy Mother.

JOHN 19:18, 25-27

I grieve for thee O Mary, most sorrowful, in the martyrdom which thy generous heart endured in standing near Jesus in His agony. Dear Mother, by

123

thy afflicted heart, obtain for me the virtue of temperance and the gift of counsel.

Pray
One Our Father and seven Hail Marys

VI. The Sixth Sorrow: The taking down of the Body of Jesus from the Cross

Joseph of Arimathea, a noble counsellor, came and went in boldly to Pilate, and begged the body of Jesus. And Joseph buying fine linen, and taking Him down, wrapped Him up in the fine linen.

MARK 15:43-46

I grieve for thee, O Mary most sorrowful, in the wounding of thy compassionate heart, when the side of Jesus was struck by the lance and His Heart was pierced before His body was removed from the Cross. Dear Mother, by thy heart thus transfixed, obtain for me the virtue of fraternal charity and the gift of understanding.

Pray
One Our Father and seven Hail Marys

VII. The Seventh Sorrow: Jesus is Placed in the Tomb

Now there was in the place where He was crucified, a garden; and in the garden a new sepulchre, wherein no man yet had

been laid. There, therefore, because of the parasceve of the Jews, they laid Jesus, because the sepulchre was nigh at hand.
JOHN 19:41-42

I grieve for thee, O Mary most sorrowful, for the pangs that wrenched thy most loving heart at the burial of Jesus. Dear Mother, by thy heart sunk in the bitterness of desolation, obtain for me the virtue of diligence and the gift of wisdom.

Pray
One Our Father and seven Hail Marys

After the seven prayers, we conclude with the following:

V. Pray for us, O Virgin most sorrowful
R. That we made be worthy of the promises of Christ.

*****

THE ANGELUS PRAYER

The Angel of the Lord declared to Mary:
R. And she conceived of the Holy Spirit.

Hail Mary, full of grace, the Lord is with thee; blessed art thou among women and blessed is the fruit of thy womb, Jesus. Holy Mary, Mother of God, pray for us sinners, now and at the hour of our death. **Amen.**

Behold the handmaid of the Lord:
R. Be it done unto me according to Thy word.
Hail Mary...

And the Word was made Flesh:
R. And dwelt among us.
Hail Mary...

Pray for us, O Holy Mother of God,
R. That we may be made worthy of the promises of Christ.

Let us pray
Pour forth, we beseech Thee, O Lord, Thy grace into our hearts; that we, to whom the incarnation of Christ, Thy Son, was made known by the message of an angel, may by His Passion and Cross be brought to the glory of His Resurrec-tion, through the same Christ Our Lord.
Amen.

REGINA CAELI

V. Queen of Heaven, rejoice, alleluia.
R. *For He whom you did merit to bear, alleluia.*

V. Has risen, as He said, alleluia.
R. *Pray for us to God, alleluia.*

V. Rejoice and be glad, O Virgin Mary, alleluia.
R. *For the Lord has truly risen, alleluia.*

Let us pray
O God, who gave joy to the world through the resurrection of Thy Son, our Lord Jesus Christ, grant we beseech Thee, that through the inter-cession of the Virgin Mary, His Mother, we may obtain the joys of everlasting life. Through the same Christ our Lord.
Amen.

★★★★★

PRAYER BEFORE THE STATUE OF OUR LADY

My Queen and my mother,
I come before you with joy and love in my heart. I know I am unable to love you as you deserve, but you see my heart and you know how much I love you.

I have just come before you as my mother; hold me in your arms, as you held your Son as a baby. Spread your maternal mantle over me; pray for me; help me. Be close to my side as my mother and ensure that I am never separated from your Son. See to it that I do not go astray from His love. Provide for me in my necessities and, in my moments of great difficulty, be my help, my consoler, my refuge.

Present before your Son all the needs of my life, but above all, teach me to unite my will perfectly to the will of my heavenly Father, because in His will is my peace.
Amen.

THE MEMORARE

REMEMBER, O most gracious Virgin Mary, that never was it known that anyone who fled to thy protection, implored thy help, or sought thy intercession, was left unaided. Inspired with this confidence, I fly to thee, O Virgin of virgins, my Mother; to thee do I come; before thee I stand, sinful and sorrowful. O Mother of the Word Incarnate, despise not my petitions, but in thy mercy hear and answer me.
Amen.

★★★★★

HYMNS
IN HONOUR
OF THE
BLESSED VIRGIN

SALVE REGINA

Salve Regina mater misericordiae, vita, dulcedo et spes nostra salve
Ad te clamamus, exsules filii Hevae
Ad te suspiramis gementes et flentes in hac lacrimarum valle
Eia ergo advocata nostra, illos tuos misericordes oculos ad nos converte.
Et Iesum benedictum fructum ventris tui nobis post hoc exsilium ostende.
O clemens, o pia, o dulcis virgo Maria.

★★★★★

HOLY VIRGIN BY GOD'S DECREE

Holy Virgin, by God's decree, you were called eternally;
That He could give His Son to our race. Mary, we praise you, hail, full of grace.
Ave, ave, ave, Maria.

By your faith and loving accord, as the handmaid of the Lord,
You undertook God's plan to embrace. Mary, we thank you, hail, full of grace.
Ave, ave, ave, Maria.

Joy to God you gave and expressed, of all women none more blessed,
when in mankind your Son took His place. Mary, we love you, hail, full of grace.
Ave, ave, ave, Maria.

Refuge for your children so weak, sure protection all can seek.
Problems of life you help us to face. Mary, we trust you, hail, full of grace
Ave, ave, ave, Maria.

To our needy world of today love and beauty you portray,
showing the path to Christ we must trace. Mary, our mother, hail, full of grace.
Ave, ave, ave Maria.

★★★★★

AVE MARIA

Immaculate Mary!
Our hearts are on fire;
That title so wondrous
Fills all our desire!
Ave, Ave, Ave Maria!
Ave, Ave, Ave Maria!

We pray for God's glory,
May His kingdom come;

We pray for His Vicar,
Our Father in Rome.
Ave, Ave, Ave Maria!
Ave, Ave, Ave Maria!

We pray for our Mother,
The Church upon earth,
And bless, sweetest Lady,
The land of our birth.
Ave, Ave, Ave Maria!
Ave, Ave, Ave Maria!

We pray for all sinners,
And souls that now stray
From Jesus and Mary
In heresy's way.
Ave, Ave, Ave Maria!
Ave, Ave, Ave Maria!

★★★★★

BIBLIOGRAPHY

Dr. Stackpole, Robert. What purity is, what it isn't, Part 3: Mary Most Pure, November 30, 2016, marian.org

Fr. Okami, Emmanuel. Pray without ceasing: Prayers for Various Occasions, copyright © 2020, Floreat Systems Publications, Benin City, Nigeria.

Holy Bible, New International Version®, NIV® Copyright ©1973, 1978, 1984, 2011 by Biblica, Inc.®

Magnifico, Laura. Why is our Lady full of sorrow? Published in Daily Bread, catholicfaith store.com

New Revised Standard Version Bible, copyright © 1989 the Division of Christian Education of the National Council of the Churches of Christ in the United States of America. www.biblegateway.com

Rev. Mauriello, Matthew. Mary, Queen of families, udayto.edu

Saints quotes on the Blessed Virgin Mary, whitelilyoftrinity.com

Seven prayers in honour of the seven sorrows of the Blessed Virgin Mary, ourcatholicprayers.com

The Seven Sorrows Devotion, themostholy rosary.com

★★★★★

BOOKS BY FR. EMMANUEL OKAMI

He Sent Forth His Word, Series 1: Homilies for Sundays, Year A.

He Sent Forth His Word, Series 2: Homilies for Sundays, Year B.

He Sent Forth His Word, Series 3: Homilies for Sundays, Year C.

He Sent Forth His Word, Series 4: Homilies for the Liturgical Seasons of Advent, Christmas, Lent and Easter.

He Sent Forth His Word, Series 5: Homilies for Feasts and Solemnities.

He Sent Forth His Word, Series 6: Homilies for Weekdays, Cycle I.

He Sent Forth His Word, Series 7: Homilies for Weekdays, Cycle II.

A Light to My Path: A Collection of Retreat Talks and Reflections.

His Voice Goes Forth: A Collection of Vocal Meditations and Nuggets.

Lord, Teach Us to Pray: Prayers for Various Occasions.

Pray Without Ceasing: Prayers for Various Occasions.

Seven Days Journey with the Lord: A Handbook for a Self-facilitated Retreat.

Praying with the Psalms.

What God has Joined Together: A Handbook for Marriage Preparation Course.

Whom Shall I Send: A Seven-day Journey with the Lord through His Word.

They Shall be Called My Children: Reflections and Prayers for Children.

When the Spirit Comes Upon You, Series 1: A Nine-day Reflection and Prayers for the Gifts of the Holy Spirit.

When the Spirit Comes Upon You, Series 2: A Twelve-day Reflection and Prayers for the Fruits of the Holy Spirit.

When the Spirit Comes Upon You, Series 3: A Twelve-day Reflection and Prayers for the Manifestation of the Holy Spirit.

Become a Better Person: A Thirty-day Journey Towards Self-improvement and Character Transformation

Vessels For Special Use: Practical Counsels for Seminarians in Formation

★★★★★

Printed in Great Britain
by Amazon